UNCLE MAGIC

UNCLE MAGIC

*The Life and Times of
Norman Myers*

The Book Guild Ltd
Sussex, England

First published in Great Britain in 2001 by
The Book Guild Ltd
25 High Street
Lewes, East Sussex
BN7 2LU

Typesetting in Times by
IML Typographers, Birkenhead, Merseyside

Printed in Great Britain by
Bookcraft (Bath) Ltd, Avon

A catalogue record for this book is available from
The British Library.

ISBN 1 85776 548 6

*This book is dedicated to
my wife, Pat Myers*

CONTENTS

FOREWORD

by Lord Hanson

Norman Myers, Uncle Magic, is a man who has made a fascinating and highly readable success of his life as an entertainer with a difference. This book is that of a colourful self-starter from inauspicious beginnings who drove himself to the very top of his own brand of show business.

He loves tradition which shines through his good and caring life story. Proof that goodness and an urge to work long and hard, right up to his present age of 80, can be a formula for a unique career.

After his war service, he started to hire films which he showed to children in the afternoons and to grown-ups in the evenings. From there he progressed to children's parties and to day nurseries.

His true avocation developed as he became known to London's nannies, who, in turn recommended him to others and soon he became a must for all family birthday tea parties in London's chic Belgravia and beyond.

My own recollection is of returning home for one of my sons' birthdays to find a dozen or so infants sitting on the floor in a circle, spellbound by Uncle Magic. Conjuring tricks, games ('Pass the parcel') everything to make himself loved by children, nannies and parents alike and a unique part of such celebrations. He knew every child by name and was always booked for next year at this year's party.

'Uncle Magic' is a charming tale, a microcosm of nursery life from the Royals to the just plain genteel. A gentle tale written by a gentle and lovable man. You'll enjoy it.

FOREWORD

by Robert Lacey

Children's birthday parties have a magic all their own. I think that I used to enjoy my children's parties even more than they did – and Norman Myers, Uncle Magic, was an essential part of that.

His fame preceded him. 'Are you having Mr Myers?' was the question the kids always asked each other. They knew that 'Uncle Magic' was the touchstone of a good party – and that promise on his notepaper was so reassuring: 'Mr Norman Myers takes complete charge of children's parties'.

Complete charge – and so it proved: conjuring tricks, party games, puppets, Punch and Judy, and even a little disco as the children grew older. We never actually saw the urbane Mr Myers ever give the stroppy ones a clip around the ear, but there was definite magic in the way he kept order in the most tumultuous gatherings. Memory blurs into a happy haze of jellies, birthday cake, candles, sticky fingers – and Mr Myers smiling through.

I heartily commend this cheerful and tasty blancmange of a book. By the end of it you'll find you have a party hat on your head, and a silly grin from ear to ear.

1

The East Enders

I assumed it was an ordinary appointment: another client in London's fashionable West End in the 1960s, asking for a Punch and Judy show. My colleague, Vic Weldon, and I were entertainers to the rich and famous, and we arrived at the smart London address with our usual promptness, ready to go to work. The house seemed a trifle quiet. We joked about this as we rang the doorbell of the town house, checking our watches and keeping an eye on our various pieces of equipment. As popular children's party organisers in London, we had a busy schedule of up to a dozen parties a day.

I had got a call from someone who sounded like a secretary, asking us if we could arrange a Punch and Judy show for a children's party at a certain address. I wrote and confirmed the date for a week or two later. We went along to the house, somewhere in Kensington, and asked if we had the right address. The person who answered the door said, yes, and to go upstairs.

Vic and I left all our equipment in the hall and went up to look at where we were going to work. We opened the door of the room, which was a bedroom. Then we looked across the floor and saw a man there, lying in bed. 'Oh, we're sorry,' we said, 'we've come to the wrong room; where's the party?'

'It's in here. I wanted the Punch and Judy show.'

We stood there. 'What?' we asked.

There was a famous television programme in the 1960s called *Candid Camera* in which a journalist, Jonathan Routh, would create a ridiculous situation and film the reactions of the people

1

involved. He also wrote about unusual aspects of London for an evening newspaper, and he'd decided to write about the services one could get in London, if one was in bed.

Quite honestly, I can't remember if we put on the show or not, because we were too astonished. The man told us he was Jonathan Routh, writing an article which argued that, in London, you could get anything you wanted, just by picking up the telephone. And he paid for everything because he got it from the newspaper.

As a rule, I prefer a *real* children's party with my other regular and more predictable clients.

I was born on the eighth of November 1920 in Whitechapel, in London's East End, where the cockneys are born. My parents were very decent and kind. They never earned much money but we always went to school clean and tidy and we were well-liked by the neighbours.

Modest though my early circumstances were, I grew up knowing family love and moral support, community ties and true friendships.

Whitechapel is the very heart of London's East End, lying south of Shoreditch High Street, Houndsditch, Aldgate High Street and Tower Bridge Approach and extending westwards to the River Lea. It has always been an area where communities have thrived, expanded and, finally, moved away to other parts of London, only to be replaced by another colourful community. At the end of the nineteenth century, when my father, Phillip Myers, arrived in Whitechapel with his family from Manchester, the Jewish community was firmly established in London's East End.

Nearly three million Jewish people fled the pogroms of Eastern Europe between 1881 and the Second World War and settled in the East End. They established a supportive community for themselves with housing and work opportunities, particularly in the garment trade. After the Second World War, the children of these families settled in north London, in areas such as Golders Green and Stamford Hill, and the Bengali community has now replaced the Jewish one with similar close-knit families and a capacity for hard work and study in order to better themselves.

2

I was born in a two-roomed flat and into a family that would, eventually, number six. I was the third of four children: three boys, close in age, followed by a girl nearly six years later. My place of birth and family home was 231 Brady Street Buildings, Durward Street, E1. The building no longer exists but was built as one of, what was called at the time, 'the four per cent industrial dwellings'.

It was the philanthropists, such as Lord Rothschild and other Anglo-Jewish wealthy people, who built a number of blocks of flats, such as the ones in Durward Street, to be rented out at reduced rates to their compatriots. They didn't like their people to live in slums. The buildings were built at the end of the nineteenth century, probably about 1890. There was only one bathroom for the whole building.

Of my grandparents and their origins, I know relatively little. My father was born in Manchester in 1875 and was named after his own father. He married comparatively late in life, and had me when he was about 46 years old. In an era before adequate social security, when many men died before they reached their fifties and left their wives without the means to keep a family together, this could have been a worrying situation for my mother.

My grandparents probably came from Eastern Europe, but they were already in England when my father was born. He came south to London when he was hardly out of boyhood. The most interesting thing is that he was a very well-read and educated man. Self-educated.

Unfortunately, in those days, working-class parents had little or no money to pay for their children's education beyond the minimum level, and many children were pushed into a trade as soon as they reached a working age so they could contribute to the meagre family purse.

They made him into a cobbler, mending shoes. When I knew him, by the time I knew what was going on in the world, he'd become secretary to four Jewish societies. He went around collecting money for charity societies. He was paid about ten bob a week, that's fifty pence now, for each one and that's how he earned his £2 a week.

My father came from a large family of 13 children. He was

about the third or fourth born, but I have no idea what kind of jobs of work the other children took on because my father never discussed the family's history or background. Except for about two of them, we never communicated much with the family in those days. We were mostly amongst our own friends and people in the block of flats we lived in. This close and supportive community in the East End was to be my family during my formative years.

Although my father was a Mancunian, my mother, Leah Myers, hailed from London. This is the sad part: she was one of three sisters and they were orphans. One sister never married, another of them married very late in life, and my mother was, for a long time, the only one who was married, and that was reasonably late. Her husband was about 40 and she must have been about 28. She was the only one who had a family. I have no idea how she supported herself before she was married. I only know that she was a wonderful housewife, and that was the most important thing to me.

Her early years were a real *Peg's Paper* story. The three girls were orphans. One of the sisters was 'put out' at 12, or 14, as a maid, nanny or home help or something in a Jewish family. She looked after the eldest son, almost like a nanny, and she was called 'Nurse'. She's still called 'Nurse' by the Cooper family today, even though she's been dead for donkey's years. She lived with this family all her life and, by coincidence, the child she looked after married and had one child, called Patricia. And that child is my wife.

This aunt, who had taken care of Pat's father all those years ago, used to come to us in Brady Street on a Friday night, for the Jewish family get-together. We used to have a ceremony and all the rest of it, and my mother used to make a very nice meal.

The Cooper family can be traced back to the eighteenth century. I have traced them back to about 1800, with family pictures and photographs, and even further. They were a very old English family, connected with the City; they were alderman and that sort of thing. My sister, who was six years younger than me, became very friendly with Pat. They were the same age. But I never knew Pat, I'd never met her – until I came back from the war.

4

The other aunt was very intelligent, and also self-educated. She was a librarian for many years in the East London Library in the Whitechapel Road, next to the Rivoli cinema, which is now a mosque, I think.

I have no idea how my parents met. They didn't seem to have any interests in common that I was aware of, but they were certainly very happily married. My father used to do a tremendous amount of reading and nothing else, and my mother was a house-wife. In this way, they lived in harmony in their two-roomed flat with their four children.

I recall my father seated in his armchair, reading. We only had one room for all of us. I remember him as a frustrated intellectual. He used to write letters for some of the most important men in the country. When these men were young and wanted to go to univer-sity, and before they became lords of the land, my father used to write letters for them. He was a brilliant man. But he was never able to satisfy his own ambitions, and that was very sad. He never talked about the cards that life had dealt him. He was a very quiet man and didn't talk much at all. All I remember is he seemed an old man, even when he was in his forties. I don't remember him any other way.

My father always smoked a pipe. He spoke very slowly and had a pipe in his mouth the whole time. Just like my brother, who died in December 1999; he always had a pipe, too. My father's pipe was always lit in those days, for his birthday, we used to buy him about a quarter ounce of tobacco, which was about one and six-pence. Today, you'd probably buy him a pound; the whole thing's entirely different!

He had a sad face, because he was frustrated. He should have been an educated man. He should have gone to university – in those days no one went to university, except the few – but he should have gone on to higher education. He would have been brilliant. His only pleasure was betting sixpence, that's $2\frac{1}{2}$p, on the races, occasionally; that's about all.

My father lived to a good age, considering the hard life he'd had, and died aged 74 in 1951, from heart trouble. My mother died at the same age, from the same sort of thing, in 1958. They remained Londoners and East Enders all their lives, but I have one big regret: they never lived to see us make a success of our lives. It's very sad.

My parents were not particularly religious. They belonged to the Orthodox side of the Jewish religion but they never went to the synagogue or anything like that. Just as people don't go to church today. But they observed the Friday meal. We had kosher food. We don't at home, today. We don't eat pork or that sort of thing but we're not fussy about where we get the meat; my parents were. In those days everybody went to special shops – there were lots in the area.

They were tiny shops. We used to buy a ha'pennyworth of this and a pennyworth of that. We buy a lot of smoked salmon now. We buy it in pounds; one pound at a time and it's gone. I remember, I used to go into a shop with sixpence and get the scraps of skin, or mixed biscuits that were broken. It was like that in those days. We had no money. But we weren't unhappy; we had a very happy childhood.

We lived in this area – we used to call it 'The Buildings' – and, every season, there were different games and things to do. It was a most amazing thing. A very happy childhood. Whereas today, the children are not allowed outside. My grandchildren are 13 and 17, and they're not allowed to come and see us by themselves. Very sad.

My father used to go around the houses and get people's pennies and tuppences to join what they called 'the charity societies'. In the East End of London, in those days, there used to be organisations which had been set up for Jewish people. They used to pay their tuppences and get food at a certain time of the year. My father was secretary of about four charity societies. One of them was called Somech Noflim, which means either helping the poor or helping the sick.

We four children were close but had quite different characters, even during our childhood. Leonard Paul, the eldest, was born in 1917 and I remember him as the leader. The next boy, Sidney, born in 1919, was a happy child, very sociable. He used to have a lot of friends, boys and girls. He was a great socialiser. One thing I

6

remember about him was he used to smoke on the side. He came in from school one day, when he was about 12 or 14, and put his lighted cigarette in his coat pocket and put the coat in the wardrobe, because he didn't want my mother to know he'd been smoking. Of course, the coat smouldered in the wardrobe. There was a hell of panic. But that was my brother. He was quite a character! He was a very good dancer, too – entirely different to the rest of us.

I was interested in the Boys' Club. My brother Sidney went there too, but he was more interested in his friends and his dancing and his girls.

My sister, Pearl Frances, was born in 1927. I didn't know her much when we were children. She had her own friends. And I didn't mix much with her once we grew up. An age difference of six years can be a lot to a young person.

As I was growing up, she was too young for me and when she was older, I was away in the war. She had a very happy and sweet character; she was a charming person. Fortunately, she met a very nice man and got married in Israel. She'd gone out there for a year and met the young man there. Then she came back to London and had a son. Unfortunately, she became ill with cancer and died at the age of 37.

What Pat – who was the same age – thinks happened is that when my mother died in 1958, two months before my son was born, the shock of her mother's death triggered the breast cancer that took her. Pearl had been very close to her mother, very close indeed. Then she had two years of pain before she died.

It was a terrible tragedy. She never did anything wrong – she was a saint, a most beautiful girl. She'd been married about 14 years; her son was 13 years old when she died. He's now living in Canada and has a very good career. He's very successful in computers and has a computer programming company. We go over and stay with him in his big house out there.

Most of my religious instruction as a child came not from my family but from the Brady Boys' Club where I spent so much of my spare time. The chap who led it, whose name was Sam Ansell, made sure we knew what was going on in our religion. We used to have Friday night services there, if I wasn't at home. Of the members of my family, I only remember my uncle and aunt as being very religious. This was the librarian aunt, my mother's sister, who had married late in life.

My childhood interests and hobbies were mostly connected with the Brady Boys' Club. I did try to play the violin for a bit, later on, when somebody at the club suggested we all play something, but it didn't last very long. I wasn't any good at that sort of thing!

I went to the local school, Robert Montefiore. There was no school uniform in those days and I came home for dinners; at least, when I was young. But I don't remember my father, although he was a voracious reader, reading to me or encouraging me to read during those school years. He was very laid-back, very quiet. He just kept himself to himself. He used to do crossword puzzles and I remember, once, he won a prize in *John Bull*. It was a dictionary. But that was about all. He never opened his mouth, really.

It was my mother, Leah, who was to have the most influence on my life. My father was negative, so I deduce she must have been positive. She made sure we were all clean and tidy and went to school. And she made sure we did what we should do at school, and she was very pleased, of course, when we got our scholarships.

I remember taking a number of scholarship exams. There were several different schools in those days: there was Davenant Foundation, Raine's, Grocer's – there were about five. They were all City of London grammar schools. Four of them were in the East End and one of them was in Hackney. I passed for Raine's Foundation, in Arbour Square, Stepney. And, as far as I can remember, that was the best school. It was almost a public school. It was about 400 years old and we had to wear a uniform there. It had a lot of tradition. The school continues to this day, but has moved its premises to the country. I think it was evacuated in the war and I don't think it ever came back. I went up there once, and I think it's now part of London University.

I only vaguely remember taking the scholarship exam, but I do remember being very pleased when I was told I had passed. But I don't think my parents were more than generally satisfied with my academic achievement. It wasn't like that in these days. I know today, for instance with my grandchildren, they go mad on exams and all the rest of it. My daughter's very keen and very interested in seeing her children get on. But it wasn't like that then. I won't say my parents weren't interested; they were very pleased when it happened. Their second child, my brother Sidney, never got the scholarship. I think he carried on at Robert Montefiore School until he left school altogether. Sidney became a barber in the East End, remaining near his friends and family, but my easy-going brother never had the ambition, or the money, to own his own shop.

Holidays, in the twenties and thirties, were not the organised event they are for families today. The only holidays were the Boys' Club. We never had a holiday at home. I went away once; it must have been when I was about ten, to Watchet in Somerset. That was through the Children's Country Holiday Fund, a Jewish organisation that sent children to holiday places. I support it now because I was looked after in those days.

However, I don't remember seeing a Punch and Judy show or playing any of the kind of games with which I was later to entertain more wealthy children. We just used to go for walks. I remember the Alabaster Cliffs at Watchet, and that's about all. At the Boys' Club camp, of course, on the Isle of Wight, we used to do a tremendous amount of things; the same things we did at the club. We used to do PT in the morning, then we had inspection for the tents – everything had to be army-style. We used to have everything: games, competitions, football, cricket, deck tennis, table tennis, all sorts of things. Then we used to have discussions, and music. For the discussions, one of the senior young men in charge, who might have been about 20 years old and down from university, would talk to us and we'd tell him what we thought about the subject. We also had very good drama classes; I enjoyed them. I think I was 'third soldier with spear' in *Macbeth*. I never had a singing voice but I was interested in Gilbert and Sullivan and I was once in *The Mikado* with the club, and I knew every word. I don't think we ever put the show on but I used to go to all the rehearsals!

It was through the club that I developed my great love of music, which I still have to this day. We used to go to the Proms before the war, when I was about 15, and other concerts, which I can't get my daughter's children interested in, at all. My wife and I still go regularly to concerts. Not so much to the Proms now, but we go to the theatre and concerts. We have the Kenwood concerts near us but we mostly go to Holland Park, where they have a magnificent open-air theatre which is covered over. They have about eight concerts every year and we go to about six of them. Opera is one of my favourite kinds of music and I have nearly every opera on tape.

Brady Boys' Club was my university. I threw myself into every activity. The drama productions included Shakespeare, and I was in most of them. We still go to see them all, and go to the open-air theatres.

I was also one of the original 'Friends of the Globe' theatre and went to its opening performance. What upset me was they'd made such a fuss about everything in the theatre being exactly as it was in Shakespeare's time. Even when they built it, they didn't use nails. They made such a fuss about authenticity, and I agreed with them. And then I went to the first show. And they put on *The Two Gentlemen of Verona* in modern dress. I was furious – I hate this sort of thing. I wrote them a very strong letter and they replied with their excuses, and I cancelled my membership. But I was, originally, a very keen supporter of the Globe, because I'm a traditionalist.

Pat and I go to a great number of the new shows in London, but I don't like 'kitchen sink' drama. We go to most of the musicals. We went to *Copenhagen* the other day, which was very abstruse. It was about Niels Bohr, the scientist. Very complicated, but it was very good. We've seen most of the shows in London now: *An Inspector Calls* by J.B. Priestley and many others.

* * *

I don't think my father fought in the First World War. He would have been about 40 when it started. But my wife's father was one of the few cavalry officers who fought in the Great War. He won medals and, somewhere, we've still got the helmet that saved his life when a bullet passed through it on the Somme, or some such place. He had three of his friends around him and they all got killed. He survived it all, and lived until 1977. He was 80 or 82 when he died.

Before the war, my father-in-law went to the City of London School, which was a very good fee-paying school, even though the family lived in Cazenove Road, N16. Both my father-in-law's maternal and paternal grandparents owned public houses in the City of London, one in Houndsditch and the other in the Minories, and, therefore, were connected with the City. I've got photographs of Pat's father's grandfather. He was, I think, an alderman of the City of London. He might have been Lord Mayor, if he'd lived. To journey from north London, every day, to the City of London School would have been too far. So as a boy his father-in-law lived with his grandfather during the week and went home to his family at weekends.

Both my father-in-law and mother-in-law were born in 1896. They were cousins and were a very close family. My father-in-law was a very good sportsman. He loved cricket and football, horse racing and boxing, you name it! He had his own greyhounds; he was a great betting man. When I say a betting man, he wasn't a gambler. He knew exactly what he was doing. He used to back the Grand National horses at the beginning of the year, say at 30–1 or 20–1, or whatever it was, and towards the end of it, they used to be down to about 2–1. He was an amazing chap. He was also a great Spurs supporter; the whole family were. It was a family sport in those days. About six or eight of the men used to go on a Saturday afternoon. And my grandchildren are Spurs supporters now.

Pat's father was a successful businessman and owned a firm that manufactured men's clothing. It was based in Bethnal Green and called L. Isaacs and Co. My wife went to quite a good school and was quite well brought up, and when I met her she was living in what I would call 'the posh part of London', Willesden.

* * *

11

There was certainly a strong sense of community in the Brady Street Buildings in Whitechapel. You used to be able to go next door and borrow some tea or a cup of sugar and all that sort of thing. Everybody knew everybody else and, the beauty of it was, being a kind of enclosed area, all the children played together – dozens and dozens of children. There was a sort of sunken path between the buildings, quite wide – about 20 or 30 feet – which was the playground area. The fourth building wasn't a block of flats, it was a warehouse for wool. In those days, horses and carts used to come along with all the wool and go into the warehouse. And there, we used to play football, because nobody minded, that's what was so wonderful! People could always see you, and you weren't afraid of anything. We had a most marvellous youth. In fact, lately, I've been trying to arrange a lunch because I've met half a dozen people from Brady Street Buildings of the 1920s. I met some through the Brady Street Club; I'm still connected with that. It's amazing; it's like an old school organisation, or like Oxford or Cambridge. The ties have remained right the way through life and we have an Old Boys' Association.

The Brady Street Club was created by people such as the Rothschilds and the Sebag Montefiores and other Anglo-Jewish philanthropists. When the immigrants arrived from Eastern Europe, they settled in the East End of London. A lot of them were in sweatshops, trying to make a living. The East End was very crowded and the Jewish philanthropists were worried: they didn't want people to become criminals, as often happens today. So, they built boys' clubs as well as flats.

There were clubs in the area in different buildings, large and small, which the children of the immigrants, especially the young immigrant boys, used to attend and where they became more anglicised. Of course, they also went to school, but in the clubs they were overseen by young university graduates. These young men, who were only five or ten years older than the boys, came from the wealthy families in Kensington and Chelsea and Knightsbridge and gave their time to the boys in the clubs. They used to mix with us. They'd play football and rugby and have discussions with us and organise drama. The discussions would be about any subject under the sun, mostly social things rather than politics.

It was a place you could go to when you got home from school and you'd had your meal. Then what? There was no television, no radio. You sat in one room with your parents, which was boring. As soon as you'd had your meal, you'd rush down to the club. Our club was in the same block as our flat, but there were about a dozen clubs in the area. There was Brady Boys' Club, Oxford and St George's, Basil Henriques Club, there was Stepney, Cambridge and Bethnal Green, and Stamford Hill; there were several of them. Brady Boys' Club was started in 1896. There, we met the most interesting people who gave us an education outside school education, and we used to go there every night. I used to do road running around the streets of London, we used to play football and rugby and cricket. Every year, we'd go for a ten-day camping holiday to the Isle of Wight. My parents couldn't afford much; I think the club only charged me 50 pence! They used to 'assess' you and work out how much you could afford. We always had the most wonderful time, and we've got photographs and we've got memories.

People like Greville Janner's father, Lord Barnet Janner, and his wife, Elsie – she founded the Girls' Club – those sort of people got involved. The clubs continue to function to this day but in an entirely different form. You don't need them any more. The children have got their Nintendos, they've got their television and computers. They've got plenty of money; I know that from my grandchildren. I want them to go to the clubs, but they won't go. Plus the fact that their parents won't let them go out on their own. We used to go anywhere on our own; go anywhere and do anything. But we were in the club all the time.

The club also had a 'weekend place' in the country, at Skeet Hill House near Lullingstone in Kent, where I often went as a boy before the war. After the war, I came back to the club as a manager, to look after boys in the same way as I had been looked after. I still see my youngsters. I call them youngsters but they're in their sixties now. And I still see the ones who are in their eighties, the ones who were my contemporaries ... They're still about! There's one group that meets up all the time. I don't go over there because most of them are over Ilford way. But we did have a very big meeting at the People's Palace in the East End during the Club's centenary year in 1996; about 600 people turned up. It's part of the University of London now. They have a big hall and that's where we met.

My family were poor but happy. I never had a birthday party as a child, which might go some way to explaining why, for the last 50 years, I have enjoyed organising parties for other children. My love of communal activities was fostered by the Boys' Club and my experience of managing different events grew during my time in the services, so it is easy to understand why my career took off in a certain direction after the war.

When a Jewish boy reaches the age of 13, he has what's called a Bar Mitzvah and becomes a man. And today, people spend five, ten, twenty thousand pounds on a party. I never even had a party for that. I went to the synagogue and said my portion. I must have been about the only one who never had a party.

I only went to one birthday party throughout the whole of my childhood. I remember it so clearly. I must have been about ten years old and I was so thrilled to be invited. It was a chap called Henry Fellerman; I still remember the name. I think he was a rather large boy, but that's all I remember. He lived in one of the other blocks of flats and his father was quite a 'wealthy' man, a businessman. I think he had a stall or a shop. This party was held in his flat and he paid, I believe, £1 for an entertainer – yes, they had an entertainer there! Later on, I charged about £120.

A lot of my friends who came from that area, friends I've known for 50 or 60 years, were better off than me and lived in houses. Their fathers were business people. Not everybody was poor; it's just that we were. I always remember, after the war when I started doing parties, it remained my biggest disappointment that I'd never had a party. But I never felt, as a child, that I lacked anything. I had love and affection at home and my brothers were ordinary brothers, nothing untoward.

My eldest brother was a great organiser. In those days, you could get a sixpenny (2½p) all-day ticket on the trams and buses to go all around London. And he used to take us. I was three and a half years younger than him and my brother was two years younger than him. He used to organise us and we'd spend the whole day going around London. I must have been about nine or ten, then. We were great cyclists, as well, but that was later on. I used to cycle to Snowdonia and the Lake District and other places. We could cycle anywhere in those days but, today, my grandchildren have got wonderful bikes and they're not allowed out on their own. It's very sad.

We used to go on these bus trips on Saturdays and Sundays. If we went to Richmond, it was like going to the other end of the world! You used to sit on the tram and it would go on and on. We didn't get off the bus and, for a little boy in those days, it was a long way. My parents used to get quite worried because my brother never told them we were going out. Mostly, we used to go on the trams, which had rails and a line in the middle of the road for the vehicle to run on.

After some time, I managed to save enough money to buy a bicycle. It cost me £3 19s 6d. It was a brand-new Raleigh bike and I bought it in Levy's in Whitechapel and had to bring it back home. There was the usual tram rail in the middle of the road, and I was riding across it on my new bicycle. The bike wheel got caught in the rail and somehow I twisted it. That was my first bike!

From boyhood, I have always known London extremely well. In fact, I know London backwards, upside down and inside out. All my life I have lived in London. And you can say I'm a cockney, as well, because I was living within the sound of Bow Bells!

I can count some Pearly Kings and Queens – East End 'royalty' – as close friends. They come with me to parties and I take them to the House of Commons when I do parties there.

Most of the children I played with as a child were the children of immigrants. I remember their parents having strong accents and many of them had not yet anglicised their Lithuanian names. When I was 13 and upwards and we used to go camping with the club at St Helens on the Isle of Wight, we used to play cricket against the local team. The team was led by the lord of manor, Lord Ebersham. And, in the local paper the next day was a list of the team players: caught so-and-so, bowled so-and-so. One thing stood out, which I remember it to this day: 'Lord Ebersham caught Chipanovski, bowled by Wychansky'. Those were the sorts of names they had! Wychansky is now Wiseman and Chipanovski is now Patsy Sino. In those days, they didn't change their names until the war came, or they became old enough, themselves, to change their names. Strangely enough, in America they don't change their names, but here they do because they want to be anglicised. That's how they did it.

Mostly, names were changed by deed poll. When I went back into the law after the war, one of the chaps in the office who'd been a leader in the Boys' Club and was called Charlie Zarback wanted his name changed. And I changed it for him to Charlie Spencer. And he uses the name to this day. He's quite a well-known art correspondent in the newspapers. Everybody used to change their name. I see people now and go up to them when I see them at the club annual service. I say, 'Hullo, so-and-so,' and he says, 'Oh no, I'm so-and-so, now.'

The annual Brady Boys' Club memorial service is a meeting to remember the 15–20 boys lost during the war. We just have tea and a biscuit and then we have the service and read out their names. Then we spend half an hour chatting. The most terrible tragedy was the very last V-bomb. It landed on a block of flats like ours in a place called Vallance Road in Whitechapel and killed hundreds of people, 36 of whom were connected with our club in some way. One of our club chaps, who was a pilot, was home on leave at the time and he was killed. His name was pronounced Satchajasky. He probably would have changed it after the war, if he'd lived.

Families in Whitechapel were very supportive of each other and I remember the several charities my father worked for. However poor we were, on Passover, around Easter, when we have the flat unleavened matzo bread, we used to have hundreds and hundreds of boxes of matzos, sugar, flour, eggs and other things, given to us by the societies to hand out to people. There used to be a queue a mile long, from our front door, of people poorer than us! We used to hand the food out to them. And my brothers and I used to make some money: we used to borrow a barrow and, when the people came round with their boxes, we used to put them on the barrow and be given a penny for carrying the food for them! People came from quite a distance. Whitechapel Road was the boundary road, and we lived on one side. The people who lived on the other side, Commercial Road, we used to call foreigners!

Although I came from a close and loving family, I remember getting into serious trouble once. And not with my parents. It was a terrible thing, and I am still mortified at the thought. One day, when I was about 14, I went down to the club. It was freezing cold weather. Leonard, my eldest brother, who was by this time at work, had just bought a beautiful new overcoat. He wasn't in the flat at the time and I borrowed it. When I came to collect it at the end of the evening in the club, it had gone. Somebody had pinched it. Right up until he died, Leonard told me off about it!

That was the most terrible thing I ever did. I looked for it every-where. I'd hung it up, as usual, in the cloakroom – nobody looked after the cloakroom. I might have been doing dramatics or a musical at the time, or table tennis – there was so much going on. I came back and looked at the peg and searched and searched. I was scared stiff, frightened out of my life because I hadn't asked my brother if I could borrow it. He nearly went mad! I told my mother. My brother said, 'Where's my coat?' I ran under the table!

My real participation in the Brady Street Club began when I was about ten years old. I went to what they called the Play Centre, which was a kind of grown-up nursery. And, at the age of 13, I joined the club properly. In my early years, I used to look after my younger sister, Pearl, sometimes, and take her to school. When we were younger, we Myers children all went to the same schools: the Underwood School and the Robert Montefiore School, both of which were in Vallance Road. Most of the children from our community went there and we used to walk to school and play together.

When I was about 15 years old, we moved to Hackney. But I continued to attend the Brady Boys' Club. I used to take my bicycle and go down to the East End each evening.

As in any community, the children around Brady Street came in all shapes and sizes. There were some tough children, but I was quiet and retiring. I was very shy as a boy, until I was about 14 or 15. The club brought it out of me. Then I became a great big organiser! And I organised people in the war, as well. This is why my career happened. Before that, I was a quiet person. I started school when I was about three or four years old. I've got a photograph of me when I was four years old, sitting on a rocking horse in the school. Although a quiet child, I was never a loner. I talked to people; I just wasn't forward. I don't remember needing to create my own fantasy world. I was totally committed to what was going on in the classroom. I liked school. We had very good teachers. Even in those days, at five, six and seven years old.

Underwood School was the children's nursery school and, after that, from eight to eleven years of age, I went to the school next door: Robert Montefiore – the Montefiores were very famous anglicised Jewish people and the school was named after them. I liked the headmaster there very much. I respected him, which, these days, children quite often don't! As children we were very well behaved. We wanted to learn, and the education was to quite a high standard. But I wasn't aware I was being prepared for the all-deciding eleven-plus exam until I was about ten years of age.

I think I only just scraped through. I wasn't brilliant at anything in those days. Quite a number of children did pass the eleven-plus then. For instance, out of three brothers, two of us passed, one didn't. My elder brother did. He went to the Davenant Foundation, which was a very good school in Whitechapel. A lot of people from the East End, and from my area, became very important people and did very well in life. That's the most amazing thing! They had the urge to better themselves. They were helped by the intelligent people in the community who brought things out in them. It was a wonderful thing. Mostly, today, that doesn't happen.

I was reading in the paper, only yesterday, about Mickey Duff. He was a famous boxing promoter. He was a Brady Boy. Bud Flanagan was a Brady Boy. Flanagan, the famous entertainer, was certainly a local hero. But he was before my time. He was much older than me – he'd be about 120 now!

It wasn't necessary for Whitechapel children to become famous to get on in the world. People became accountants, barristers, solicitors, doctors, businessmen, and all sorts. People I know now live in very nice places and a tremendous amount of them came from the East End. The Asian community is similar to this, today. They all work hard and, like the Jewish people, they have a close-knit family; education is the most important thing to them, because it's the only way you can get out of anywhere, and that's how it happens.

Although it is about 70 years ago, and I can no longer remember the teacher's name, I can remember my primary school master as being an excellent teacher. We used to respect him very much indeed. He never took the cane to us. It was only later, in the other school, that they did that. I used to walk about a mile to school every day, and back again, sometimes with other children and sometimes on my own. We had a respect for education; we used to like going to school.

Although I was not one to push myself forward in my younger years, the characters of my brothers and sister were quite different to mine. My eldest brother, Leonard, was completely independent. He liked doing his own thing. He got a job when he had to go out to work, and he loved to travel. He used to do a lot of cycling and, just before the war, he was going to cycle around the world. His project was advertised in the paper and had his photograph taken. He got as far as Turkey, just as war was about to break out. I think they thought he was a spy. They arrested him and put him in jail but he managed to get out after about a week. I think he said he worked for the Bata shoe company; it was the only company he could think of that was international! They'd taken his bike, of course, but he got to Italy and got a lift on a motorbike all the way to Dover.

Leonard joined the Air Force at the beginning of the war, in 1939. He became a corporal and a technical instructor at the RAF station in St Athens, in South Wales and he never came back to London. But Leonard wasn't a man to push himself on people. He was like my father in that respect. Not ambitious. When he married, I understood, if he made just enough money to live on, he was happy. He was a sales representative but, much later on, he studied chiropody and became a chiropodist for the last ten or fifteen years of his life. He was very interested in first aid, and he was a commandant in the St John's Ambulance Brigade for about 30 years.

We were all growing up fast, and life was carrying us with sudden speed, in very different directions.

2

The Organiser

I did a tremendous amount of cycling in my youth. From the moment I bought my first bicycle, at about 13 years of age – the one that got caught in the tramline – I used to cycle everywhere, including to the Boys' Club after we moved to Hackney when I was 15. I also organised the cycling group at the club. The 'kids', who are now about 70 years old, still come up to me and say, 'Remember when we went to Snowdon? Remember when we went to the Lake District?'

We used to cycle there and back again, as well as touring the area. I was a great youth hosteller, and I used to cycle out to the country at weekends. In those days, I think it used to be about a shilling a night, which is 5p, and about 7d (3p) for lunch. I know that when I went to the Lake District on my own for 16 days, I had under £4 with me – and I had a wonderful time!

When I was about to go away, I'd say, 'Dad, can you give me any money?' And he used to put his hand in his coat pocket, and if he brought out sixpence, sevenpence or eightpence in coppers, that was all the money he had. So I never expected any financial help from the family. My father was never able to save money or invest, but I believe he did his best for the family. I'm not complaining, at all. We had a very happy family life.

As a boy, I wasn't a great football fan and I didn't become interested in cricket until the war, when I formed the Bahrain Cricket Club, but I liked rugby. We got them to play rugby at the Boys'

Club, and I played rugby at school. It was our game and I enjoyed it.

My position on the field at school was fly half. I was a little fellow. In fact, I was tiny! I remember playing other schools but I was never in a top team. I wasn't that good at it; just an average player. It wasn't until the war that I realised I had potential, and, of course, at 14 or 15 when I started organising the cycling section at the Brady Boys' Club.

But my life was changing. I had to leave school when I was 14 because my parents couldn't afford to keep me there. That was my biggest tragedy. In those days, I wanted to be a teacher. I realised that, after about a year at my new school, when I was about 12. I enjoyed the teaching at the school: it was to a fantastic standard. The teachers were marvellous. I thought if ever I was going to do anything, that was what I wanted to do.

I didn't have a particular subject I was interested in, I just enjoyed them all. I was one of these average boys. I was never anything special. If we had an exam and I got 55 or 65 out of 100, that was fine. But our English master was good. I remember him so clearly, a chap called Shivas. I think it might be his son who does production at the BBC, because it's a very unusual name. This literature master taught us very well and he gave us a love for Shakespeare and good books. He got me interested in P.G. Wodehouse, and I used to love the Greek legends. I wish my grandchildren were interested in them, but they're not. It's how I got my knowledge of Greek mythology: I read every one of the stories. It was probably the fantasy side of it that I enjoyed: Odysseus and Hercules, Cyclops and the rest of them. I learned Latin at Raine's. That was what was so wonderful, coming from the East End of London, from Whitechapel, and here we were, doing public school subjects.

I used to walk to school in Stepney every day, which took me about 20 minutes. And we used to have to go all the way to Beacontree in Essex, which was about ten, fifteen or twenty miles away, to play games at our playing fields. We'd go there for an afternoon and play rugby. There weren't any showers. I used to come home on the underground in my dirty and stained clothes, get out at Whitechapel and go home and give all the stuff to my mother to clean in the room! I also remember playing tennis and kicking a football around the playground.

Raine's Foundation was a large school, but it had a tiny playground. It was very old, like a public school – it was about 300 or 400 years old – and must have had 400 or 500 pupils. The masters used to be in gowns and mortar boards and the boys wore school uniform. I particularly remember the headmaster, a Mr Dagger – a very important chap. And we had very good science laboratories; I remember the smell! And we used to go from one room to another for each lesson. A lot of my friends there went on to university.

Literature was the subject that remained a favourite of mine. Maths, I wasn't all that wonderful at. We used to have masters saying, 'You multiply by this and you stick in the middle twice the subject.' I remember that. It was an equation ... the master used to have a bit of chalk and lick it with his lips. Those are the sorts of things that stick in my mind. I was also very interested in history and geography, but world, or even European history was not yet considered important or useful. In those days it was all English history.

When, at 12 years old, I decided I wanted to be a teacher, I had no idea I would have to leave school two years later. As my fourteenth birthday approached, I realised my parents couldn't afford to keep me there. They said, 'You know, you're coming up to fourteen and you'll have to go out to work.' It was very sad because at 16 you took the matriculation exams. But I didn't feel hard done by. It was normal in those days that, unless you came from a financially better off family, you had to leave and go out to work. My eldest brother, Leonard, who'd also won a scholarship, had also left school at the same age.

Leonard had found a job in Houndsditch, in one of the many wholesale warehouses for which the area was known. He just went in and got a job, and that's where he changed his name. His name was Leonard Paul Myers, and when they asked him his name and he told them it was Leonard, they said, 'We've already got two Leonards here. What's your other name?' He told them it was Paul, and, right up until the day he died, he was known as

Paul. Leonard Paul became a salesman in a shop and, when he moved to Liverpool, he took a job as a travelling sales representative for a ladies' garment manufacturing company. And, finally, as I mentioned before, he became a chiropodist.

It was in 1934 that I left school; roughly two years before the war clouds began to gather. But I still attended the Boys' Club nearly every night for table tennis, drama, discussions and road running. We used to run for about an hour, on average, once or twice a week. We ran round the streets of London for three or four miles with some of the managers who were much older than I was, in shorts. And we used to have road running races once a year.

Jobs were not advertised in the papers in those days. People found work by asking for work. My aunt knew someone who worked in a stockbroker's office and I was sent there to apply for a job, probably as an office boy, as I had no qualifications. But my lack of physical size was a disadvantage that day. They said, 'You're much too small for this job!' and they wouldn't employ me, so I went out and walked up and down the City. I saw a notice saying 'Office Boy Wanted' for a solicitor's office on the corner of Fenchurch Street, just opposite the station, and I went in there. They offered me 50 pence a week, which I took, and I started work there. The money I brought in helped my mother to keep us going. I was given one and sixpence ($7\frac{1}{2}$p) back, to last the whole week. Sixpence used to go on the cinema, sixpence on chocolates and sixpence on fares.

As a boy, I had enjoyed the cinema. When we were very young, about six, seven and eight, we used to go to the cinema and sit through the programme three times around! We used to go in at about eleven o'clock and my mother used to come out and find us. We'd still be sitting there at six o'clock in the evening. There was a cinema called the Foresters, in Mile End Gate, which was very close to us. The films we children saw were the ordinary films for adults. In those days, there weren't any films you shouldn't watch. We used to see all the Charlie Chaplin films, Laurel and Hardy and the Three Stooges. I enjoyed those. Later on, I was to collect these films as part of my job but, at the time, I had no idea I was going to go into children's entertainment.

The films were 'talkies' – the talkies started in about 1928.

24

Mostly, as a boy, I used to go to the cinema on my own. It cost fourpence in those days, which is under 2p. I was absolutely in another world. It took you out of yourself. The cinema was, of course, very popular in the days before home entertainment. There used to be about 12 cinemas in our area. Even here, in Finchley, where we live now, people tell me there were about six, eight or ten cinemas. They've all gone! The Foresters was a favourite cinema but there was also another one, called the Rivoli, in Whitechapel. It's now a mosque I believe.

By the age of 14, I was totally involved with the Boys' Club, and the cinema was less attractive. It's unbelievable to imagine how much these clubs taught people of our age, and took us out of our surroundings. It was like going to public school, in a way, because you met people from a different background who were very kind, and not condescending. There was no condescension from the young men who volunteered to help at the clubs. They were more like school prefects; they used to take you out and they were wonderful to talk to.

At 14, I had left school but I had only just begun at the Brady Club. I used to work, come home and have my supper and go to the club. I was with Brady from about ten years old until I went to the war, when I was nearly twenty.

The firm of solicitors I joined was called Courts and Company. In fact, my solicitor today – not the same firm – is the nephew of the person who ran that company. The firm was on the first floor of a bank, and I appeared on my first Monday morning in the suit I'd been given for my Bar Mitzvah. I think it was Burton's – 'the fifty-shillings tailors', they were called. I was very smart. I'm not sure if the suit was striped. And I used to get *The Times* every day to look important! And I always used to read it – I've always read the papers, I've always been interested in what's going on – but I was very City-conscious!

Courts and Company was a small legal firm. My duties were, at first, running around, taking letters here and there and going to the bank. At the end of the year, they gave me a rise of half-a-crown, which is 12½p, and I felt a bit disgruntled. So I found another job with a solicitors called Herbert Baron, in Queen Victoria Street, where they paid me £1 2s 6d, which was a lot!

The new job was far more interesting. I was a junior clerk and I used to go to court with the future Lord Chancellor, Quintin Hogg. In those days, I think, you only paid about two guineas for a barrister. Quintin Hogg was about 30 years old and had just started practising as a junior counsel, and my boss used to employ him for practically every case. A barrister had to have someone to go with him to the court, and I used to go nearly every day with Quintin Hogg, whether it was to the High Court or the City. Barristers never came to the office; I used to meet him at the court or at his office at 5 Paper Buildings in the Temple. I used to hold the papers and give them to him. During the cases, I just sat there.

When a writ was issued, the name of the Lord Chancellor was always on it. The name of the Lord Chancellor at that time was Douglas McGarel, Viscount Hailsham – Quintin Hogg's father. In those days, it used to cost £1 10s (£1.50) to issue a writ; today, it's much more. I used to deal with a lot of writs and I knew Quintin Hogg's father was the Lord Chancellor: there was a lot of cachet attached to him. In the end, we were full members of the same club, the RAC. In fact, I recently 'lost' £35,000 because I retired from the club before I should have done. But that's another story.

I found the cases absorbing. The whole atmosphere of the Law Courts was interesting. I used to know every back alley-way, all the secret passages to use. We used to issue writs in the Law Courts. I'd go there for the firm and, if I had an hour to spare, I'd wander around, going from court to court, listening to cases. You could go anywhere you liked. But this was not the situation years later.

My boss after the war, David Geller, had a car and I had learned to drive. We used to drive to the Law Courts, park the car in there and do whatever we had to do. This must have been around 1947. Then, a few years ago, I had a case at the High Court; one of my clients owed me about £600. I drove to the Law Courts, got to the gate and the man said, 'Yes, what do you want?' I said I had business at the Law Courts and I wanted to park the car. He said, 'You can't park here, it's only for judges.' I said, 'I always park my car here. I've been coming here for years, since 1936. They've always let me park here!' The security man laughed so much that he let me in.

It was the theatre of the Law Courts, the drama and the tradition, that impressed me so much, and the history. In fact, I've been going back there recently, until last year, because of a charity for barristers with which I was connected, The Edward Bear Foundation. It was to do with muscular dystrophy, and we would meet in the downstairs cafeteria of the Law Courts. I did the parties for the charity and they made me a member, so I used to attend their meetings.

Before the war, I wanted to be an articled clerk. But, in those days, that cost a lot of money. Today, they pay you to learn. In those days it cost hundreds of pounds and only wealthy people could afford it. My plan was to watch and wait. I enjoyed my job as a junior clerk: the cases were fascinating and I moved about the City, and the people I worked with in the office were also very interesting. I was sent to the County Court, as well as the High Court. In the County Court, I sometimes used to take documents and speak up for the company. If it was a case involving money, I used to present the facts for the judge or the registrar, so they could decide for or against.

I worked in the legal profession from 1935 to 1940. My first year was spent in the office of Courts and Company, the next two years in the employ of Herbert Baron and, finally, the first years of the war with David Geller. David had been an articled clerk in Courts and Company, then qualified and started his own firm and asked me to join him. Again, I hoped to become an articled clerk. His father was very wealthy, through property. When David qualified, his father bought him an office in Fore Street, which is where the London Museum is now, near the Barbican. David had an office there until a bomb dropped on it in 1940. The whole of the City of London was flattened and everything in the office was lost, all the records. We had to start up again in Dean Street after the war.

*　*　*

I was now a managing clerk and had more responsibility in the office and with court work. I used to go to the courts quite a lot. Outside work, I used to read adventure stories: Henty, *Treasure Island*, and other stories. It's difficult to overstate just how much we youngsters of that generation depended on our clubs for a good selection of books.

By this time, I had started studying for the law exams. I used to go to the Regent Street Polytechnic at Oxford Circus, after work, and study. I was always trying to better myself but I found the classes very tiring every evening. It was long way to go, and to save money I used to walk. It used to cost fourpence on the bus from Oxford Circus to Whitechapel and I might save a penny by walking to Holborn, and another penny by walking to somewhere else. You could get a couple of bars of chocolate with that! It's hard to believe today, and when I tell my grandchildren that, they're amazed.

I also economised by taking sandwiches for lunch instead of eating in a café or a restaurant. I couldn't afford to go out to lunch. Nor did I start the day with an enormous breakfast. I'm not a big eater, in any case. Even today, I only have cornflakes and a slice of toast. I'm not a breakfast eater.

Going to the cinema was now a thing of the past. I studied for two years, from the age of 16 to 18, before having to give up. I wanted to do it, but it was too much. Quite a few of my friends from school took accountancy and articles because their parents could afford to put them in. Full-time work took its toll on my professional studies and I channelled my energies back into the Brady Club.

The suits I had to wear to the office were purchased for about £2 10s and lasted about two years. I didn't wear a hat but I carried a briefcase. The qualified solicitors wore pin-striped suits but it wasn't the Edwardian era of stiff collars. People were very kind in the offices. When I worked for Herbert Baron, he insisted on having coffee at eleven o'clock in the morning at the café around the corner. He always took me there, even though I was a boy. And when I worked with David Geller, we used to go to Valerie's patisserie, which was in Soho, and have coffee and a cake.

I don't recall any particularly cold winters in the late thirties. I would do, because we had no central heating at home. We only had one fire in the sitting room and the bedroom was freezing cold – I remember that. The sleeping arrangements in the tiny flat at Brady Street were my parents in one room with my sister, Sidney and I together in the other bedroom and Leonard, the eldest sleeping in the lounge on the sofa. It was all very difficult.

When we moved to Hackney, we kept the same sleeping arrangements. It was only two bedrooms again. In fact, I don't know why we moved. When I see my grandchildren, they've all got their own rooms, their own computers and televisions. We had everything in the one room. They don't know how lucky they are!

Even the kitchen in the new flat in Hackney was the same size as the previous one. But I remember' my mother's cooking very well. The favourite dishes were chicken soup and chicken. They were a great delicacy. We had one main meal a day and my mother, like all women in those days, did all the housework. I recall her using an old mangle to wring out the washing. It used to be in a tiny area called the gate, which was a small open area just in front of us. I have no idea where she did the washing or hung it out to dry.

My mother was a sweet, pleasant and homely woman. After the war, I took a lot of movies and I had her put on video. Although she was ten years younger than my father, she died only seven years after him, in 1958. She lived alone in Hackney. Pat and I had moved, by then, to a flat in Maida Vale, and she used to come over to us quite often and we used to take her home. But she wanted to be independent and she wanted to live on her own. She was never lonely: she had the support of her friends and family and the community around her.

My father had died of a heart attack in 1951. I can't remember his death, at all, but I do remember my mother's. She also had a heart attack. She was taken to Hackney Hospital and I went to see her, and when I got back to the office I found out she'd died, and I went straight back to the hospital.

*   *   *

I never experienced any anti-Semitism myself when I was a boy or a young man. Never at school, never during the war. But I knew there was trouble brewing. I knew there were boys and men who used to go into the streets and counter-demonstrate against the British Union of Fascists, led by Sir Oswald Mosley after 1932. Mosley's crowd used to use a lot of violence in the East End. It went on up to about 1936 and the Battle of Cable Street.

For a long time, the police were on Mosley's side and, unfortunately, the politicians were on his side to the extent that they didn't stop his activities. They used to wear the uniform of the Nazis, brown shirts. Mosley and his followers used to march, purposely, in the East End of London, where the Jewish people were, and daub anti-Semitic slogans in the streets.

On October 4, 1936, when Mosley and 3,000 of his followers decided to march right through the East End. That was enough for the Jewish people, and especially for the Communists, in those days. And the dockers, who were very tough, were on the side of the Jewish people, as well. They put barriers across the top of Cable Street, which is the top part of Whitechapel and Aldgate, and waited for Mosley to come. There was a big fight! Over twice that number of police tried to clear the way for the Fascists, with baton charges and mounted patrols. They were met with a barrage of bricks and stones from 100,000 East Enders, chanting the slogan of the Spanish Republicans, 'They Shall Not Pass'. The police had to stop the march and send Mosley back to where he'd come from. That was the turning point, like the Battle of Alamein in the war.

The Battle of Cable Street was the moment when the Fascist movement's popularity in Britain took a distinct dive. Mosley was interned soon after World War II began and was only released in 1943 because of illness. I had friends who were involved in sabotaging Mosley's hostile, paramilitary demonstrations, but I didn't know about their work until after the war. Even the event in Cable Street: I wasn't involved in that, at all. I didn't even know it was going on. I should have been involved, in hindsight, but I wasn't.

I had friends who were high up in the movement against anti-Semitism. There was an organisation called 'The Forty-Three Group', who used to go out and obstruct the Fascists, and counter-demonstrate. In fact, after the war, when it happened again, the solicitors I worked for used to have to send barristers to defend the people who'd been arrested. But, before the war, I was a busy teenager with my mind on other things.

The family were now settled in Navarino Mansions in Dalston Lane, Hackney Downs. I didn't enjoy living in that part of London as much as I'd enjoyed the close community in Whitechapel. But I made four good friends there. We used to go to each other's houses and listen to music and talk. We shared a love of classical music, Tchaikovsky, Beethoven, Handel and Mozart. You'll see, later, how this all came out during the war!

We used to listen to records, the old 78 rpms. I didn't have a gramophone, myself, but I used to go to a friend's whose father owned a greengrocer's shop, and was therefore comparatively wealthy, and he had a record player. The chap's now a very big estate agent. We also used to play a lot of Monopoly, an excellent training-ground for all aspiring estate agents.

Concerts were beginning to play an important role in my love of listening to music. I used to be taken to them by some people at work. The articled clerks used to take me to Henry Wood's Promenade Concerts at their original venue The Queen's Hall, just by the BBC in Portland Place, and then I used to go to the Albert Hall. And in the Boys' Club, some of the wealthy patrons had permanent seats at the Albert Hall, or a whole box. I used to organise groups to go to the Albert Hall. I would tell Jim and George and John from the club they could go this week, and Bill and what's-his-name they could go next week, and we used to go and sit in a box and listen to the Proms. All free. It was wonderful.

A friend of mine, the Hon Philip Samuel, his father Lord Samuel was Home Secretary in Lloyd George's Government, who died recently at the age of 95, had two permanent seats at the Albert Hall. He used to take me there quite a lot. But I never went to the Last Night of the Proms – it was too exciting – but I've got it on tape. We always had proper seats: boxes or permanent seats. I got to know the Albert Hall extremely well, and probably went to a concert once a fortnight or once a month. The Royal Festival

Hall, built after the war in 1953, is another concert hall that Pat and I now enjoy going to. In fact, yesterday afternoon, we were at the Purcell Rooms for a matinee.

*   *   *

Sometimes, I brought my friends from Hackney Downs to the Boys' Club. One of my friends was to become a journalist and to write an interesting autobiography about the street where he lived in Hackney. We used to have social dances at the Brady Club, once a week. But my brother Sidney was more that way inclined than I was. He used to go to the dances at the Palais and all that sort of thing.

The Sunday evening social dances were held either at the Boys' Club or the equivalent Girls' Club. In about 1936 or 1937, or 1938, the Boys' Club closed down and we all moved to the Girls' Club, so it became a mixed club. I used to go to the socials, but to stand around and watch, mostly. I used to dance sometimes and I had a girlfriend. We learned to ballroom dance: the waltz, the quickstep and the foxtrot. I used to enjoy dancing, but I didn't do a lot of it. The young couples would hold hands, perhaps, but that was all. It was nothing like today. I mean, there must have been a lot of people who went further than that, but not me. My brother probably did!

I don't remember ever taking a girl to the pictures – I probably couldn't afford it. I was quite normal, I think, but not forward.

Although my social life was undergoing some changes, I always used to observe the Friday evening meal before going to the club. We used to eat dinner at night. My mother always gave me a meal when I came home from work. I often went away at weekends, usually going cycling and to youth hostels, or I would simply go out for the day. I was one of the few people who never stayed in bed in the morning. A lot of people used to go out dancing on a Saturday night and come back and get up at twelve the next day. But I used to be up at seven or eight, as I do today.

3

Music and Movement

I was working for David Geller when I received my call-up papers. My two brothers had joined the Territorials before the war, so when the war started, on 3 September 1939, they were both called up. Sidney went in the Army and Leonard into the Air Force. I was younger than them and was called up in 1940. I went up to get my number in Cardington, Oxfordshire, in October that year. Cardington was a big old RAF establishment, where they used to have the airships. I joined the Royal Air Force, which I entered the following year, in March 1941.

I was already psychologically prepared for war. Everybody of my age was ready for it. In those days, all the youngsters were expecting to be called up and were waiting for it, or volunteered earlier. There was no question of not wanting to go; we all went. It was our ethos, I was sent to Blackpool, where I started my square-bashing. I went into the wireless section and had to learn Morse code.

Six or nine months before I had joined the Air Force, I'd joined the Home Guard. The beauty of it was they taught me Morse code. The result was I knew the Morse code up to 12 words a minute before I went into the Air Force. When I joined the force and we were learning the Morse code, which we had to do in six weeks, I had six weeks off! I used to go and report in the morning, then go on the beach at Blackpool or on the pier, because I knew it all. This was in March, April and May of 1941. It was a very pleasant time. The beach, unlike the south coast, was not covered in barbed wire.

From there, my group were posted down south, to a further

33

training centre in Calne, Wiltshire. We used to call it the sausage village, because it was where they made the sausages. After our training there, we were sent to Bournemouth and, in June 1942, we were posted overseas. We didn't know where we were going. We just had to report to our base and we were sent up to Liverpool, on the Wirral. The next day we were bused to the docks and put on a big troopship, *The Stirling Castle*. It was carrying 5,000 Army chaps and 500 Air force. Although the ship was very crowded, we were lucky and didn't have any work to do; the Army did all the hard work on the ship. I chose the Air Force because it was more elite in those days, and also because I wanted to be a flyer. I applied for aircrew training but, as I discovered later on, out in Alexandria where I was supposed to take my course, I had bad eyesight. Which can be taken as a good or bad thing. I'm still here. A lot of my friends didn't have bad eyesight and didn't survive the war.

I began my war service far away from all the people I had known in London. I was on my own completely. But, going back to the club experience, I was well-versed in meeting people and socialising. There was never any problem with that and it was very pleasant. I soon made new friends.

It was on the troopship that I learned to gamble. I was very naïve in those days. We had about a hundred Australian Air Force on the ship and they were so mad on gambling, it was unbelievable. They played a game called 'two-up', which I watched and learned to play. You get two coins and throw them up in the air and if you back two heads and they come down two heads, you win. If you call tails and they're heads, you lose. Sometimes, some of these chaps could throw the same sides six or seven times. It's a real Australian gambling game. They're absolutely mad about it, even today.

Without mishap, the troopship landed in Freetown, the capital of Sierra Leone, situated on a rocky peninsula at the end of a range of wooded hills. The natural harbour was an important naval base in World War II.

It was the first time I'd seen Africans. I saw them carrying coal on their backs and it was frightening, in a way, to see these enormous people, almost like slaves. It was very hot and they were bare-backed, carrying huge sacks of coal up the gangway to fuel the ship. It looked cruel.

The ship moved on to South Africa. We landed in Durban. We were very lucky because we spent about five weeks there, instead of one week. Normally, you spent about a week there, then most people went on to India. Of the ones who went up to India, most of them got caught in Singapore and were made prisoners of war. Just our little lot was sent up to Egypt. I was now part of a wireless unit of about 30 or 40 airmen – Forty-four Wireless Unit, it was called. We arrived in Cairo, in Egypt, and went down to Suez, then six of us were stationed 200 miles south of Suez, in a tent in the desert.

Before my posting, we enjoyed ourselves in Durban. We had a wonderful time. The Forty-four WU was billeted in the RAF's Clarewood Camp, but there was a Jewish club in Durban and the Jewish boys migrated there immediately. We were looked after magnificently; taken in as part of the family. I met a Jewish girl there; I might have married her. Marjorie Levy was her name. My wife and I tore up her love letters after we got married!

I courted Marjorie for five or six weeks, which was a long time for a relationship during the war when young people were being parted at a moment's notice, never to know when they would meet again. I wrote when I went north, but it wasn't that strong a relationship. When I say we might have got married, it probably wouldn't have happened. It was a typical wartime romance in which people were thrown together for a limited period of time. It wasn't serious, at all, and the friendship petered out before the war ended.

The Forty-four WU arrived in Cairo and we were immediately sent to our headquarters in Suez. Then we were sent all over the place. Some of the unit went to Aqaba in Jordan; I was sent to Ras Gharib in Egypt, in the southern Arabian Desert.

I didn't mind the desert, although I didn't find the scenery beautiful; it was very different from Whitechapel. But I enjoyed it. We were free. I like open air and I liked the life. It was free and easy, and I became a rebel in that I don't like discipline. I soon got used to the temperatures. I had no problem in the whole of the war. The only affliction I ever got was out in Iraq where I got sand fly fever for a couple of weeks, but no malaria or anything else.

Our small unit of six men in the desert had the job of tracking German aircraft. Just before we got there, a German plane came up from the south and we had to warn our HQ in Cairo if any more planes were coming. We kept surveillance with our binoculars and if we saw anything, we had to send out a Morse-coded message saying, 'Enemy approaching.' But disappointingly, we never saw anything.

We had never met before going on the troopship but, happily, we all got on well together. One of the men a chap called Stan Bransbury, was about ten years older than us so he became a father-figure. A very nice chap I kept in touch with him until he died ten years ago.

The unit remained in the desert for approximately four months. In October 1942, Montgomery's troops began the Battle of Alamein and marched on to Tripoli, beating Rommel in the western desert. Our unit followed Monty. We never saw any action, I must admit. We arrived at Tobruk, on the Libyan coast, and took a plane to Tripoli. What we did see, however, was the carnage and destruction that had been left by the fighting. I've still got photographs which we took from the air of the burnt-out planes.

We arrived in Tripoli and spent Christmas in a tent in Castel Benito. But we were not short of diversions: we used to go into Tripoli for pleasure. It's a beautiful town.

None of us ever had any doubt who would win the war. We knew we'd win. There was no problem with that. There was never any other thinking; we couldn't afford it.

We spent almost a year in Tripoli. And this is where the rebellion happened. My friend and I were a bit anti-discipline. We had a warrant officer who made us pull our socks up, because we were wearing shorts, and we always made certain our socks were down. This sounds like a very small sort of protest, but what happened after that changed the whole of my life.

From Tripoli we thought we'd be going through North Africa, round to Italy and on home. We hadn't been home on leave; we hadn't had any leave, except in Africa. But because we were against discipline and against pulling our socks up, our warrant officer got so annoyed with us that he posted us all the way back to Egypt and down to the Persian Gulf! This proved, against all odds, to be the turning point in my life.

My wartime service in the Persian Gulf was the most wonderful two years. We flew down to Egypt, then I was sent to a place called Habbaniyah, which is 50 miles from Baghdad. There was an enormous RAF base there, a magnificent place with theatres, swimming pools and everything, right in the middle of the desert – 113 degrees in the shade. Then I went on to Bahrain, where I spent the next two years.

Even though I wasn't promoted at all during the war – somehow I managed to avoid it – I had a wonderful life. I played bridge for four hours a day and I organised the Bahrain Promenade Concerts. James Wakelin was the British Council man in Bahrain. He and his family and I became very great friends. I arranged, with his agreement, that I'd take troops of all ranks, sergeants and officers, to his home once a week. He had a beautiful apartment, very English in decor, overlooking the Courts of Justice, and I put on a promenade concert for everyone.

The concerts were my idea, from going to the Proms in London before the war. I got the equipment by indent: the gramophone, the music and all the rest of it. I used to put a notice up on the boards in the various messes and we'd pick up the other rank, sergeants and officers and take them in a three-ton truck to my friend's home. There, we'd have tea and coffee and it was all very English. In a way, the men were all very homesick.

I used to put on a record, an overture or a symphony, and continue with other music. There were about 20 or 30 people sometimes less – whoever wanted to come. The concerts were popular because they got people away from camp.

Next to be organised and arranged was the Bahrain Cricket Club, according to MCC rules. I indented and we got all the whites. There was a welfare side to the RAF and we used to have welfare officers. I'd give them a list of what was needed and they'd issue it. For the cricket club, we got all the equipment we wanted. It might well have been donated by volunteers in England who were concerned for the troops' welfare. But I don't really know where it came from. Either they bought it, or they got it.

The Bahrain CC, decked out in whites, played against the Oil Company XI and the Cable and Wireless XI, as well as local people. We used to have wonderful matches. I was captain and club secretary. And that was my war!

James Wakelin was great friends, through his work, with a number of sheikhs, including the Sheikh of Bahrain, and I went hawking in the desert with the Sheikh of Bahrain's nephew, who was then about 14 years old. I think he became the Sheikh of Bahrain and died recently. I wrote to the family and sent them some of my photographs, but they never answered my letters.

I kept in touch with James Wakelin, though. We seemed to click, and got friendly. We spoke the same language and found each other pleasant company. We saw each other with our families, back in England, but James Wakelin died a few years ago. I spoke to his wife, about a year ago. She's much older than me, and she's in a home now. His son, Timothy, who was two years old when I first knew him, must be about 55 now, and I've got movies of him playing with Jennifer, my daughter, when she was two or three years old.

I was in Bahrain from 1943 until late 1944, serving in the wireless unit in the Persian Gulf, combing the skies for enemy aircraft. We were in touch every day with HQ. We used to give weather reports to other places, like Sharjah. There were wireless units dotted all around the Persian Gulf and we used to swap weather reports and any other information and it was all sent back to HQ in Cairo. Sharjah is very famous now because of the international cricket competition held there. We worked four hours on, and eight hours off every day. That was our shift work. In our spare time we had to do something and somebody taught us bridge, and I have loved playing bridge ever since.

On our way back to England in October 1944, we went back to Egypt first. Then we took a Polish motor vessel, *MV Batory*, from Alexandria. It was new in those days; I think it's still cruising around now. I came home with a friend, and we were also bridge partners. Today, if I play bridge for money, I will only play for a small amount such as 3p a hundred. In those days, 50-odd years ago, we played for sixpence a hundred and, in the five days my friend and I were on the ship, we cleaned up. We did very well indeed. It was a lot of fun!

Although I have never really been a smoker, I was a social smoker in those days. But only because they gave us cigarettes. They used to issue us with tins of cigarettes and I came home with 2,000. At one stage I tried smoking a pipe, but I didn't really enjoy it. My elder brother, Leonard smoked a pipe for the whole of his life.

I finally arrived back in England in October 1945. It was freezing cold. What upset us was that in May 1945, when the war ended, we were still in Bahrain. There was a possibility that, instead of coming home, we were going to have to go out to the Far East to finish off Japan. I didn't want that, I wanted to get home. I hadn't been home for years. Lucky for us, and I still think it *was* lucky for us, they dropped The Bomb. And that stopped that war, and we came home.

Back in England, I still wasn't finished with the RAF. They sent me up to somewhere in the wilds of Norfolk. Freezing cold! As I was waiting to be demobbed, I considered this latest posting a great waste of time. But the war was over and they had to put you somewhere. Everybody had a number which depended on when you'd gone into the services and your age. When my number came up, I was out.

I got my demobilisation papers and I had to go to Wembley to get a suit; they gave every serviceman a suit before he went out. I don't think the suits were particularly good ones, but Pat's uncle was in charge of dishing out the suits, so I got a reasonably good one. Still, the moment I arrived home, I went out and had a suit of better quality made to measure.

It was not until May 1946 that I was finally demobbed. I was fed up being where I was, and I wanted to be home, so I pulled a few strings. James Wakelin, the British Council chap who had been such a good friend in Bahrain, had a brother who was a group captain at Bushey Park in Teddington, London. Through Wakelin, I got in touch with his brother and he transferred me to his post. That meant I was able to be at home. I used to get a train every morning, all the way to Richmond. I had a bike at Richmond and I used to cycle to Bushey Park, where I used to just mess around until I was demobbed.

The RAF took five years of my life. I went back to David Geller, the solicitor I had been with until I was called up, and continued working for him. David had remained a solicitor during the war. He was so unfit, he was obese. In fact, he died of obesity, unfortunately. He was only two or three years older than me but he died very young. He was a very nice chap.

David Geller's office had been bombed in 1941, while I was still working for him, and the practice had moved. In fact, I was in London for quite a bit of the Blitz. When we lived in Navarino Mansions, in Hackney, we had a little shelter, just outside. And most nights, before I was called up for the Air Force, we had to go down into this horrible, dank shelter for several hours while the Germans bombed all around us. And, in the morning, we came out and found half the streets were flattened. It was a frightening experience, but it didn't worry me. We didn't think it was going to affect us. You just felt frightened.

My wartime experience had changed my outlook on life and I could no longer see myself as a 'nine-to-fiver' for the rest of my life. It was having been out in the open. I didn't want to be in an office all the time; I got fed up with that. I worked for David Geller for another year before our working arrangement changed completely. With my boss, I started a film business called Home Films. It was a significant step towards my eventual career.

Again, it was a wartime experience that had put an idea into my mind: seeing films in the desert, projected onto a screen in the open air. In Bahrain, there was nowhere else to go, so we used to have an open-air cinema. The RAF sent down a projectionist, his equipment and some old films and we used to sit out in the open, like they do in America these days, and watch the films. All the troops came to see the films. We had the Army there, as well. We used to sit on benches to watch.

When I returned to David Geller's office, I talked about the concept of showing films in remote places with him and another office colleague, David Schiff, who had also just returned from the war. David Schiff and I both felt we didn't want to continue the office work we'd been doing before the war, and plans were laid.

We started up Home Films with a couple of vans and we employed a projectionist and went into business. We went out to a place in Oxfordshire where they had a village hall, and we showed films in the evening and charged people to come and watch.

Oxfordshire was, in fact, a random choice. After the war before television was really going, you were allowed to show films anywhere, as long as you were five miles from a cinema. So we had to find little villages, tucked away somewhere, five miles from the main cinema, and you'd say, 'Right, that's the village hall for us!'

We took over a village hall in Oxfordshire and sent the projectionist there every night to show films. We'd charge sixpence or a shilling to go in and we hired the films from the film libraries of Rank, Columbia and other big film companies, Soon additional village halls, mostly in Surrey, were hired for film shows. We even organised film shows on aeroplanes; we were the first to do that. Air Chief Marshall D.C.T. Bennett started a company called South American Airlines and we trained his stewardesses to operate the 16-mm machines. We hired out the machines and films. The first film ever shown was Dickens's *Great Expectations*.

I never used to make films, only hire them to show. Today, they have videos, but in those days, all the big companies had enormous libraries of 16-mm films. MGM had them, Walt Disney – but then you couldn't get Walt Disney, unless you had influence. You weren't allowed to show Disney films, at all. We did, in fact, but that came later.

Mostly we showed old English films. You could hire them for about £2 to £5. And we sold ice creams. We showed films to the children from 5 p.m. to 7 p.m. then the adults from 8 p.m. to 10 p.m. It was a long and tiring day. Pat and I and our operator, Mr Carter, would leave London around one in the afternoon, taking the ice cream with us and arrive back in London well after midnight. We were lucky if we made about £8 at the end of the evening.

Soon, I was showing films to children in a different situation. At about that time in 1949 or 1950, someone asked me to show films at children's parties and day nurseries, at Christmas time. I remember, we charged £3 19s 6d for the half hour and £4 19s 6d for the full hour. That's £3.95 and £4.95 respectively.

At first, showing children's films after tea at parties was just a sideline. The children's nannies organised the games for their charges before tea, but, soon, I saw there was a gap in the party market. I suggested to various members of the nanny 'mafia', as well as the children's mothers, that I could handle the whole of the party entertainment, leaving them free to concentrate on the children's tea.

Soon, nannies and mothers were discussing my party service with other nannies and mothers, and recommendation followed recommendation. As children's birthdays came round again, and those of their friends, I began to find my entertainment service more and more in demand.

4

The West Ender

I don't remember organising my very first party, but I do remember my first famous client. The great actor who became a regular client, early in my career, was Sir Ralph Richardson. His son's nickname was 'Smally', and his first party, on 1 January 1950, was so successful that I was asked to do the boy's party the following year. This time, the family wanted some games and a puppet show. My wife Pat's cousin, Neville Cooper, and his friend, both of whom were only 14 years of age at the time, put on a delightful puppet show and we were a great success.

I got to know Sir Ralph over the years. I used to talk to him at the parties. He had beautiful diction and a wonderful presence. He had a magnificent house, right next to The Spaniard's pub on Hampstead Heath, and he lived there until they finally moved to one of the houses down by Regent's Park.

When the puppet show went down so well, I realised I could organise things, party-wise, without having to do it myself. Whatever people wanted, I was able to arrange it. And that was how things started. Then I began doing the novelties. I found the children were sitting down to tea with Christmas crackers, hats, balloons, masks, squeakers, all that sort of stuff, and they always had to have a little bag of something as a going-home present. I built up a very big business on that side. I had a whole room put aside in my house, full of the different things for it. I must have got through 10,000 balloons a year.

43

At first, my helpers and I used to blow up the balloons ourselves. Then I bought a machine to do it. And I used to provide very good presents, not rubbish. I used to go to the wholesale toy warehouses and buy a gross of things at a time. Knowing the right articles to buy was part of my work.

Before I go to a party, I have no idea what I'm going to do. As soon as I see the birthday child, I've got the feel of what games I'm going to play. I know what they want. It's all there, an instinct.

At first, I didn't include magic tricks. It was not until the sixties that I began to incorporate magic in my repertoire. Before then, films were the mainstay of the entertainment.

The parties were from 3.30 or four o'clock until six I used to arrive and play games with the children for 40 or 50 minutes. I would organise the old favourites, such as, the Farmer's in His Den. Musical Statues and Grandmother's Footsteps. Then they'd sit down and have a proper tea, which used to take some time. After tea, I'd put on a film show: cartoons or whatever was suitable for the age group. And, after that, they went home. That was the way children's parties went in those days.

Later on, when the children began to expect magic tricks at their parties, I employed magicians. I was never a member of the Magic Circle but I used to know people who were, and they used to get magicians for me. But I soon found the magicians I'd hired weren't going down well with the children. They weren't any good. They had all this marvellous equipment; they had such wonderful stuff, even by today's standards, but they had no rapport with the children. On two or three occasions, I had to take the magicians off and do something with the children myself.

We used to do parties like the Hurlingham Club Picnic, with their enormous riverside grounds in Fulham, West London. We still, once a year, almost 30 years on, do their Punch and Judy show for them. It's a wonderful day outdoors, like Ascot, with thousands of people and different entertainments. We also organised, for many years, Hurlingham's Children's Christmas Parties for about 200 children and their parents. Vic and I played games with the children and showed cartoon films after tea. Then Vic would bring out his Hamilton puppet and we'd put on the Punch and Judy show, after which Father Christmas would give out the presents. We did many parties in the main house but, later on, we used a hut in the grounds for a large number of private children's parties.

In the early days, I advertised in *Nursery World* magazine and regularly had a good response. I soon got clients and my connections grew from there. Harrods and Hamleys, and other big department stores who provided a children's party service, repeated their bookings. Nannies recommended me to other nannies for their charges' parties and, soon, I was employing several people to cover my multiple bookings in London, the suburbs and country estates.

I met my Punch and Judy man, Vic Weldon, in about 1955. He rang me up one day and said, 'I hear you do children's parties; I'd like to do some.' And, from that day, he did all the children's parties with me. Vic had been in Ralph Reader's *Gang Show* entertainment during the war. The *Gang Show* was a popular radio show, an extension of the old music hall variety programme, with a regular cast of performers. There are quite a few *Gang Show* members left. Harry Secombe, who went on to the *Goon Show* and television's *Songs of Praise*, was one of them. And Vic's still going strong, too. He learned how to put on a Punch and Judy show before the war. He's a very good Punch and Judy man, and he also does games and magic and everything else, like me.

All the important parties I have organised over the last 30 years, including Hurlingham, the large charity parties at Claridges and the parties at the House of Commons for 200 children, have always included Vic Weldon's entertainment. Our friendship has lasted to this day. I'd never do a big party without him. Like me Vic Weldon is at an age when most people would have retired, long ago. He's actually a couple of years younger than me. He lives in the Chigwell area and he still does a lot of parties up there. And he goes on holiday a lot. He's married but he has no children, so he enjoys life.

Vic has been performing the same high-quality Punch and Judy show for years. For a Punch and Judy man, the show is always the same, and Vic's show is perfect. As every child knows, the show has Punch being told by Judy to look after the baby. Judy has to go away and while she's gone, Punch tries to teach the baby to walk. He gets annoyed with the baby and starts hitting it. The baby hides and Punch asks the audience where the baby is. The children call 'Yes, it is!' and 'No, it isn't!' at the appropriate moment, and start shouting and screaming and getting very excited. Then the police-man comes and they're all shouting again. They're finally asked, 'What shall we do with him?' and that's rather interesting because most of the children say 'Hang him!' or 'Kill him!' Children can be quite vicious.

It was Sir Keith Joseph, later Lord Joseph, Margaret Thatcher's Education Minister, who was unsure about the morality of the tale of Punch and Judy. We used to organise a lot of parties for his children, and he would stand and watch the show. He used to love it, but would insist that we didn't hang Punch before his children. We always had to do something else with Punch!

Some parents were more involved in the management of their children's parties than others. Often, parents would request games that were completely wrong for the occasion and I would modify their ideas. We did it our way, and it worked. Today's parties are less easy to re-arrange. There are disco parties – I've got one coming this week. I'm not supposed to be doing any more parties but I'm doing one down in Oxshott, Surrey, on Sunday for the golfer Colin Montgomery, which I'm sure will be all right.

The trouble with disco parties is that, quite often, the girls are six to ten years old. Three-quarters of them don't want to dance. It's usually the birthday girl and, maybe, one other dancing. So, you go along to these parties and the mother says, 'Oh, they love dancing!' They've got the tapes and they've put them on. The tapes are all rubbish because they're not really dancing tapes. One or two kids dance, all the rest don't. The boys never mix with the girls, they stand around and do nothing. And if you left it like that, the whole party would be a flop. I have games for every type of child and for every age of child; I can go from three years old right up to fourteen or fifteen years old, that's my speciality. I know exactly what they want and I get them to do things.

This party on Sunday is for four to seven year olds and they're having a disco. It's the whole party, except for the tea. This is what the parents think is right. But the children will do nothing and be bored. However I have the solution to the problem. What I do is say, 'Right, you like dancing? I'll put the music on, we're going to have dancing.' Two of the children do 'wiggle-wiggle', the rest of them are standing around doing nothing. So I introduce games.

Soon, the children are joining in the games; dancing and playing games. Then I do a magic show and the children are happy. Very few children want to dance today, and the boys, especially, don't want to dance at the same time as the girls. Some of them do this shaking and jump all over the floor but most of them are too shy; they don't want to do it, especially at that age. As soon as I begin the games, all the children join in, and can alternate the games with the dancing.

I did many parties in Lincolnshire, at the big houses and big estates. They were mostly for children from the ages of ten to fourteen, and were held at Easter or Christmas when they were on holiday from their boarding schools. I organised some excellent games for them and the three hours always went very quickly.

During the fifties, when I was starting out, I was averaging one party a day. Unfortunately, my records for that decade are incomplete. But, as with any new business, the turnover had to build up. For extra income, I ran the Shell-Mex and BP film library. They had an enormous library on golf and other sports, such as motor racing. For instance there used to be a lot of Young Farmers clubs around the country, and I provided the operating equipment for the films for their meetings and charged around three guineas a time. Gradually, I took over the bookings side of the operation. We were doing 10,000 bookings a year. I had an office in the Strand, which the company gave me next to Shell-Mex House. I didn't run the office myself, because I was busy doing my children's parties. But my sister and my wife and other people used to run it for me. The film bookings company was called Greville Films – I was living in Greville Hall at the time.

Pat was a tremendous help to me and was totally committed to my business. She's an extrovert in that sort of situation. For instance, Pat was at the Brady Girls' Club after the war, when we were married, and she was a manager there – one of the senior people – and she loved it

Of course, I had no idea when I met Pat that she was going to be such a wonderful partner for me. But I was very delighted to marry her. We were immediately in harmony. She loved all the things I was doing, that's the beauty of it the clubs, the parties. She took a party of 20 children to Holland on her own in 1955 or 1956. She was able to do all that.

It was in 1952 that another of my 'big breaks' arrived: I was asked to organise the entertainment for a children's party at Claridges Hotel in Brook Street, Mayfair. Lady Lowson, the wife of the Lord Mayor of London, was holding a party for 200 guests from all over the country, 100 children and 100 nannies and mothers, in order to introduce her grandchildren to society. All the children were very young; some were babies. Altogether, it was a splendid affair, and it made my name known to a large number of the right people. After that, I organised parties for many of those who'd attended.

That was my first big party. I was a little nervous when I got there. I didn't go there with any concrete plans, just a lot of ideas in my mind. I'd brought equipment for the music but the games were simply in my head. What I do, is put the music on and try and attract the children that way. I put certain music on for certain games I want to play.

I don't remember how I received Lady Lowson's commission to organise her children's party. It either came through one of the agencies, Harrods or Hamleys, or my advert in *Nursery World*.

I did many parties at Claridges after that, as well as at a lot of other large London hotels. I was now becoming well known. I did so many parties at the Hilton in Park Lane, the hotel I used to recommend to my clients as a venue, that the hotel used to invite my wife and me to dinner there, free, with all the works!

The children were certainly always very interested in my games and films. This might be because there is more participation in games and the children are totally engaged. Even in my magic show, not so much in those days, but now, children participate most of the time.

It was during this increasingly busy period in our lives that Pat and I began our family. My daughter, Jennifer Melanie, who was named after a relative called Muriel, arrived on December 16, 1953 and my son, Geoffrey Mark Leigh, on January 1, 1959. Geoffrey was named Leigh after my mother, Leah, who had died just before he was born. We employed a Spanish girl, Maria, to help them look after the children when our second child was born. She was marvellous.

We lived in our flat in Maida Vale for ten years, from 1948 to 1958, then moved to a four-bedroomed house at 80 Bridge Lane in Temple Fortune, NW.11, where we stayed for forty years. Although the house was large, a lot of the space was taken up with articles for my business. Much of my party stock remains with us still, even after moving to our retirement flat in Etchingham Park Road, Finchley, N3 in 1997.

The children took the business in their stride. I used to take my son to all the parties with the royal children. He became very friendly with Prince Andrew. I met almost all the royal children through the parties I organised. The Duchess of Kent invited me to do their parties two or three times, for example. I remember at the first party I did a magic trick. That was in 1966, for their son, the Earl of St Andrews. In 1969, I organised Lady Helen Windsor's fifth birthday party, then her sixth, after that.

In the fifties, when I was establishing my business, I gradually expanded my repertoire and services. I began to do the whole party for the children, and the nannies were absolutely delighted. And what pleased me was that some of the party-givers, like Lord Ogilvy, who then became the Earl of Airlie and Lord Chamberlain to the Queen, and who owns Cortachy Castle next to Balmoral, had six children and I organised every one of their parties. I started with his daughter, then, after that, his eldest son, David, later Lord Ogilvy, when he was about six or seven years old and I did every one of all the children's parties, every year, for donkey's years. All the other nannies used to come with their charges and, through that, I used to be invited to organise all the other parties.

49

Very soon, it wasn't advertising that was generating the greater part of my business, but personal recommendation. I had to keep my name in *The Tatler* and *Harper's* because that's what my clients used to read, and I got a lot of write-ups, but after a while, it was all recommendation.

I learned as I went along, noting the children's reactions to certain games. I knew that a particular crowd from a certain school would enjoy certain games. The private schools in London, like Hill House, where Prince Charles went, had a lot of pupils whose parents used my services, time and again. I knew the sort of set-up they'd want and I started a filing system to record the games and tricks I'd done with them.

I have a comprehensive card index system, A substantial box, crammed full of index cards, pink and white and blue, holding the records of most of the parties I have organised over the last 40 or 50 years. Each card gives the name of the person who gave the party, the date, the venue, the number of guests and guests of special note, not forgetting the games played and puppet shows. The cards are in alphabetical order.

The title of the person was always noted on the card, the address and telephone number, and the age of the child whose party it was. Most of the cards have dates recorded for each year the child was growing up and having a party. I also had a cross-reference system, in case I met the child at another party. Without the organisational skills instilled in me at the Brady Boys' Club, I would not have been able to keep track of my nationwide party service.

I also kept a note of the mileage I did travelling to my clients' country estates, because I used to charge them. In London, I'd charge them X amount for the entertainment, and if I was going to the country, I'd charge the same amount plus 30 or 40 pence a mile for my travelling. It was the time involved.

The extra information noted on a card might read: 'Met third wife and three small new children; David, two, Frederick, six, living in Monte Carlo.' I always updated my filing system after every party. I see from one card that I charged £8 for 160 miles to Bury St Edmunds. That's to Ickworth, an enormous estate, Home of the Marquess of Bristol. I think the owner's sold it now and he died of a drug overdose; very sad.

Every card in the box belongs to a person who was, or is, at the top end of British society. The address on Asil Nadir's card, for instance, reads: 80 Eaton Square, SWI, and there is a telephone number. The party dates read: 1982 and 1983, and there are extensive notes on games and films shown, for my information. He used to ask me to take his son to watch cricket at the MCC, where I'm a member. The son must be about seventeen or twenty, now. I've noted: 'Cricket bat and ball bought', and: 'Next year going to Sunningdale'. Unfortunately, the Polly Peck affair intervened. He's now in Northern Cyprus. I haven't seen or contacted him since. Another card says: 'Neville, Lady Rupert'. Her husband was private secretary to the Duke of Edinburgh. The address is Uckfield in Sussex, the year is 1956 and the card notes 'Films via Harrods'. Her husband paid me a compliment when I was down there. He said he'd heard so much about me, he thought I must be wonderful. I was so thrilled. Before one party, Lady Neville turned to me and said, 'Mr Myers, would you mind taking over the party? I'm going riding with the Queen this afternoon . . .'

Although I was advertising in *Nursery World*, the magazine which has now been replaced by *The Lady*, I found many people who wanted an organised party went straight to Harrods. They'd ask Harrods, who'd ring up somebody, and they used to give me all their children's parties. Hamleys, the top London toy store, also gave me their children's parties. In fact, when I was charging five guineas for my parties (£5.25) which I thought was reasonable, Hamleys were charging their clients eight guineas and paying me the eight guineas! I used to get wonderful parties from them.

I did parties for Hamleys for many years, until, unfortunately, they employed a person in their magic department called Ali Bongo, who's now working with the TV magician Paul Daniels. He took over Hamleys' parties and that's when I stopped getting business from them.

On another index card, I noted for 1970: 'No Royals at the party.' This, of course, was not always the case. On the same card, for 1968 I wrote, 'All Royals.' That was over 30 years ago. Since then, I've done a lot of second-generation parties.

These children are now the Countess of this and the Duchess of that; they've all married. There were eight Royals who attended children's parties in the late sixties they were Prince Andrew and Prince Edward; Princess Margaret's two children: David Linley and Sarah Armstrong-Jones; the Duchess of Kent's two children and Princess Alexandra's children, Marina and James. My diary for 1965, now a battered leather book, bursting with yellowing pages, shows that I was managing three or four parties every day, and, towards Christmas, I was doing thirteen or fourteen parties a day.

The organisation needed to handle this volume of business had to be precise. I had to have equipment, the men and I had to sort out where they were going. I didn't realise, until I looked again in this diary, just how much I was doing. And that was just one of the years.

By the mid-sixties, at least a dozen people were working with me. I'm a hundred per cent man, and what happened was, I started building up the business, and then I discovered I wasn't getting a hundred per cent from all my people. Some of them were very good, one or two of them weren't and I was getting a few complaints. I don't like getting complaints. So I began to slim down my operation, gradually, until there was only Vic and me and two other people who I relied on, one of whom was Paddy Ingram, who, like me, specialised in games and magic and films.

But I had been planning to create a large organisation. In 1965 while other people were relaxing and enjoying their holidays, over Christmas and the New Year, my colleagues and I were dashing about London, and further afield, to and from the town houses and estates of the rich and famous. There isn't a page in my 1965 diary that isn't full of appointments. From January 1, we did all the top people's parties: the Kirwan-Taylors in Grosvenor House, Park Lane, the Invalid Children's Aid Society at the Savoy, and so on, all the way through.

By the early fifties, I knew that children's parties were my future. I knew I wasn't going to do anything else. The business wasn't very profitable to start with, and I was married and starting a family.

Tea time at large party catered by us

My 'Magic Box Trick' (2 bricks fall off a solid wire)

House of Commons
children's party
Paul Daniels and me

Helping hand in cutting
birthday cake

Prince Andrew at 5 years old at Tennant (Glenconner) party

The Brougham children among my very large balloons

Deborah Brougham's Disco party

Cutting the cake ceremony

Lord and Lady Lever's 3 daughters
Annabel, Isabelle and Yasmine

But as I was doing parties in the afternoons, I was free in the mornings. I'm not one to sit down and do nothing. Someone said to me, I think it was Pat's father or uncle, why don't I become an agent for a clothing manufacturer and go around selling their clothes in the morning and continue with my parties in the afternoons. Which I did, and I was soon earning quite a lot of money. That was how I managed to keep going.

One of the clothing firms was M. & N. Horne, in Clerkenwell, where they had a big clothing factory. I was introduced to them and they liked my attitude and my style. They were manufacturers at the cheap end of the market. My father-in-law's firm was at the top end: Harrods and all the rest of them. The firm gave me sample trousers and suits and I used to call on shops, credit firms and other organisations and try to sell ten or twenty garments. I built up a nice little clientele, and, at that stage, the garment business was more lucrative than the parties. It was real money; that's how I was able to live.

It was ten years before the party organisation was solid and successful enough to support the family. But I persevered. During the fifties, I was juggling several different jobs at the same time to make ends meet. I sold clothes in the morning, gave parties in the afternoon, ran the Shell-Mex and BP film library, showing films at the agricultural clubs and, of course, helping to manage the Brady Club in the evening. But I was always most comfortable when I was busy. It was what I wanted, and I thrived on the workload. I was young, I was in my thirties. It was more work, not less, that carried me forward.

One day, I received a phone call on behalf of Mr Randolph Churchill, Winston Churchill's son, asking me to give a party for his daughter, Churchill's granddaughter. This was one of my first parties – I believe it was a commission from an agency, such as Hamleys or Harrods. These big stores were a valuable source of business, but, on one occasion, they put me in an awkward situation.

I remember it was a family who owned a chain of stores which are a household name in this country. We took some photographs; in those days we provided a lot of different services to earn extra money. We used to take photographs at the party for the client and send them on later. Our prices were reasonable, but I think this particular person never paid me. I couldn't get the money and so I didn't bother about it any more. The following year, I rang up this client, as I normally did, to ask if they needed my services, and the lady said No, she'd got something else arranged.

I had a drawer full of follow-up cards and always rang my clients and reminded them I'd organised their party the previous year. People liked to be reminded, and we'd send a card to them a month or two before the party date, when they were starting to think about things. After I'd phoned this woman, Hamleys rang me and asked me if I'd do a party for Lady somebody; it was the same person. We did the party and I think she was a little bit upset because we came along. But the party was a success and there was no problem; I didn't ask her about the outstanding bill.

The third year, the same thing happened. I sent her a card and no, she didn't want a party. But, that year, I think Harrods asked me to do the party. So, for three years running, I did a party for the same people, through different agencies, when they didn't particularly want to hire me again!

I don't think it was because these people wanted to ring the changes on their party entertainment; I think they were embarrassed. They hadn't paid me, that was the point. I don't think it was the entertainment because the children certainly enjoyed it.

The fifties, and the sixties had a traditional feel to the children's parties. Most of them took place in the clients' houses in locations like Eaton Square. I usually organised them in SWI, SW3, SW5 and SW7, the King's Road and all the turnings off there; Kensington, Chelsea and Knightsbridge. In those days, people hadn't gone across the river, which is the situation now because of the price of property. In those days, the children's party-givers used to live in Chelsea Square and Cadogan Square, Sloane Square and all around there.

The other important place was Chester Square, which had the most magnificent houses. Baroness Thatcher lives there now and there are a lot of Americans, but in those days, it was full of English aristocracy. Harold Macmillan's daughter lived there, in a wonderful house, for donkey's years, and the Campbells lived there. But Chelsea Square, I think, had more aristocrats per inch than any other place there was.

What pleased me, when I visited the top people's houses in the 1950s and 1960s, was the clients' straightforward attitude to a children's party. They always allowed you to use their best dining room, and they let you go up to the drawing room: magnificent rooms with Aubusson carpets and superb furniture, and they didn't mind. The nannies and the mothers used to come in and sit and watch you do the entertainment. But, at the parties in the suburbs, such as north-west London, north London and south-west London, during this same era, the people were nouveau riche.

I don't want to sound class-conscious, but these people used to have lovely houses and they'd send you right up to the top floor, to the playroom. They wouldn't dare let you into their beautiful lounge because the children would put their sticky fingers on the walls, they said. But the children wouldn't have done that. I used to say, 'If I'm there, nobody does anything wrong, at all.' Because, as I said, I used to do all these parties at the top places and they didn't mind where we were. I hated being sent up to the playroom. Downstairs, in the sitting room, there were the grown-ups, sitting, drinking, eating or whatever it was. It was an entirely different social scene; but most interesting.

Another facet of the top people's children's party circuit in the fifties and sixties which I enjoyed was the opportunity to meet future clients. It was how I built up my connections. My wife, in those days, never came with me to the parties because she was looking after our own children. It was mostly me, on my own.

At the end of the party, I used to pack up all my equipment and stow it in the corner, and the father of the house would come home from the City or elsewhere, ready to relax. We used to sit down together, for an hour, probably, have a chat and a glass of whisky. We became great friends and built up a rapport, and that's why I used to go back to the same families, time and again. Men like Tiny Rowland – we used to discuss politics and business. He treated me as an equal. He was a wonderful chap. Another client was Sir James Goldsmith: I used to sit down and smoke his cigars and enjoy his whisky. They were marvellous people with tremendous personalities. I used to love to sit down with them after the parties.

And I enjoyed being with their children, just as much. At teatime I preferred to stroll around the room, cup of tea in hand. I didn't slope off and have a cup of tea somewhere else. I used to be with the children all the time, just in case they threw a jelly, which they rarely did. Prince Andrew did, once, but that's another story!

The lead-up to a children's party could take several forms and always required meticulous planning and execution. If the call came from the people themselves, it would be the nanny, usually. She would say something like, 'Oh, Mr Myers, young James is having a party on the twenty-third. Are you free?' And I'd say, yes, if I was, and, if not, we'd try to arrange another date. Then I would write the family a letter of confirmation. I was always very strict about that, because of my legal background. It always set out exactly what I was going to do at the party. I had to do that, because, a couple of times, I had to go to court. Fortunately I only had disagreements with one or two of my clients.

In the normal course of events, I would ring my client, two or three days before the party, and confirm the number children I was to entertain and any other requirements the person might have. If they wanted presents, I'd confirm that, and the catering, we did everything. Pat used to take care of the food. We did a lot of catering for the children at Aspinall's, the Clermont Club and places like that. A typical menu was, first of all, the crisps and twiglets, the nuts and bits and pieces, all round the table. Then there were freshly made cucumber sandwiches, cheese sandwiches, egg sandwiches and ham sandwiches, beautifully cut up – and masses of them on the plates. And lots of chocolate biscuits and so on. We used to give them an enormous amount of food, far too much, but we liked doing it that way. And we charged a very reasonable price. The people enjoyed themselves, and we got a profit out of it.

For years, Pat and I used to cater for the same people. Pat prepared the food at home, with a friend. She had several people she could call on who would come along in their spare time and help. They used to like coming to the nice houses! In fact, years ago, Pat's mother and aunt used to help at the parties because they liked to see inside these houses. It's an entirely different world.

At first I was slightly in awe of the houses I visited when I first began to organise children's parties. You used to go into these splendid dining rooms, and there were staff; it's what you used to read about. But, after a while, I got used to it and it was normal. After about a week!

The birthday cake was a most important item to consider. I found out who did the best cakes in London. They used to make them for Harrods – Gloriette's in Montpelier Square, Knightsbridge. I got very friendly with them and they quoted me, with a big discount, what they used to quote Harrods, so I made a nice profit. The cakes were magnificent: any type or shape or size. They could be airships or balloons. The best one was a fairy castle with four wonderful turrets.

Anything the client wanted, I could arrange. I used to do a lot of parties at 30 Pavilion Road, which belongs to Searcy's. They're the top caterers in the country. They cater for the Royals and we used to have some royal parties there, as well. It's a lovely town house, with a ballroom and everything.

At one stage, we used to do ice cream cakes from Harrods. I used to go to Harrods about an hour before the party, pick up the ice cream cake in its box – it was full of dry ice – and take it to the party. You couldn't open the box because of the ice. You used to put it on the table and open it at tea-time, and it was wonderful.

I remember once, we ordered an aeroplane, a beautiful aeroplane. The boy whose party it was particularly wanted this aeroplane. And when I opened the box, it was a revolting mess; they'd forgotten to put in the dry ice. The poor boy was most upset.

Arranging the cake, the pièce de résistance of a party, could be a tricky business and not something that always went according to plan. We used to do a lot of parties for Michael Heseltine's children. He had two daughters and a son and we did all their parties. In fact, I'm still very friendly with them. His eldest daughter wanted to come to one of my parties recently, just before she got married. She's a journalist now They were charming to me and I used to make all the arrangements for them, the food and the lot, in their house in Wilton Crescent. The first party I did for them was when Michael Heseltine was the Minister for Air. Fortunately, on this occasion, I did not arrange the cake.

Michael Heseltine had just come back from India on the Concorde, and he'd asked an airline chef to make a Concorde cake for the party for his son, who was about five or six years old. The *Daily Express* was there, taking photographs. I organised the party, provided all the other food and arranged the games. And then it was time for tea. I used to make quite a ceremony out of a child's first moments with the birthday cake. I've got a magic candle which livens up the proceedings. We were ready with the cake and I put the candles on it. We blew the candles out and we all sang 'Happy Birthday'. I gave the boy the knife and he started to cut the birthday cake. And, to everyone's horror, we realised it was cardboard. It wasn't a cake at all. They'd made a cardboard cut-out of the Concorde!

We also provided the drinks for the children. Mostly, we used to give them orange juice. We used to have soft drinks of all kinds, such as lemonade, Coke if they wanted it, but most of the nannies wouldn't let them have Coca-Cola. After the sandwiches and chocolate biscuits and cake came the jellies; we never gave them ice cream. And, before they came down to tea, the children had their games and the little prizes.

The order of play for an afternoon party ran something like this: I and my helpers, if I had help that day, would arrive about half an hour before the party and get everything prepared, well in advance. If I was preparing the novelties and blowing up the balloons, it would be one hour beforehand.

If the party involved catering, Pat and her helpers arrived with me, two hours in advance, and started preparing the tables for the children's tea. We took the tableware, including the knives and forks. If we did the catering, we did everything. The clients didn't want to arrange anything, just sign the cheque at the end.

Money wasn't something the parents of these children normally worried about. In the two or three hours preceding a birthday party, I invariably found my clients had been gripped by a much greater fear.

5

The Magic Touch

All major concern for the parents of a birthday child was whether the entertainer would show up: a party without an organiser meant a large number of boisterous children to look after for two or three hours. Another worry was that the entertainer would only arrive at the same time as the children, so I always told clients I'd arrive early, because there was always a possibility of a traffic jam, and arrive about 20 minutes or half an hour before the arranged time. I would sit in the car and wait until the appointed time and arrive at the client's door exactly 30 minutes before the party, as promised. The delight and relief on the parent's face when we arrived was well worth the extra effort of getting there early. At the beginning of my career, the parties were from 4 p.m. to 6 p.m. and, if we looked out of the window beforehand, we'd see the nannies and their charges walking up and down outside, until exactly 4 p.m. when they'd ring the bell.

The children were shown films in the early days. I'd set up my music with the tape recorder and tapes, and my film equipment with my small 8-mm projector and screen. Later in my career, there'd be a few magic tricks with my red magic box. If the parents had requested novelties, I used to bring hats, balloons, masks, squeakers, crackers and presents.

The presents were prepared at home, in the room in our house we had given over to party articles, such as toys and novelties. If they wanted novelties, I used to arrive at the party an hour in advance to blow up the balloons. They were very large balloons and we used to string them up and decorate the house with them.

We tied them in such a way that they were like grapes; you just pull them and they'd come down.

The pleasure the children got from the novelties I had planned and prepared became my pleasure, too. What I loved to see at the end of the party was the children going out and crossing the road, say Chester Square, with all these big balloons. I knew they were from my party and it was a wonderful sight.

I reckon 80 per cent of the time, I simply provided the children's entertainment. The moment the first child arrived, we'd begin playing games until tea-time, so there wasn't any gap in the proceedings. I found that games before tea was the equivalent of giving adult guests a drink at a dinner party; by the time they've had one drink and socialised with the others, they're more relaxed.

The important thing with the children was that they were on the go all the time, even when they'd had tea. When I gave parties at hotels, tea-time was the most terrible thing. There were enormous gaps between the courses and the children became restless and went wild. The whole time they have to be managed and entertained. I would usually spend my time going around the table, talking to the children and passing the food around or making sausage animals for them. Something has to be going on the whole time.

When Pat and I organised the children's tea, we ended the proceedings with my magic candle trick. I went to an American party in London, many years ago, where they had one of these magic candles. (I used to do the parties for President Kennedy's nephews and nieces; for Jacqueline Kennedy's sister, Princess Lee Radziwill in Buckingham Gate.) It's a candle which, when you blow it out, lights up again. I thought this was rather a good idea, but they weren't available in England. I found they were selling them in Canada, so I wrote to the wholesalers in Canada and bought a lot of them, and I used them in London and found they were a great success. I knew I'd come across another gap in the party market. Then I found out they were made in Japan, so I wrote to the Japanese Embassy; I've got a whole file on it, somewhere, with all the details. They gave me the name of the manufacturers in Japan. They said, yes, I could be the sole importer in the UK, as long as I bought £600 worth of candles at a time, which was a lot of money in the sixties. I said I'd let them know, and I went round the London stores and asked if they'd be interested in taking them, as well.

I thought I was on my way to the big time. I went to Harrods and places like that, and they were delighted with the product. Except, they weren't allowed to buy the candles because, in those days, they were considered a firework hazard. And the project collapsed. I still bought my candles from Toronto, but I couldn't become an importer myself. The sad thing is, some years later, they changed the law and somebody else brought them into the country and they were selling them all over the place. I could have made a fortune. That was one of the fortunes I didn't make. There were one or two other fortunes that slipped by me, but that's another set of stories! This was the first one, the first million that didn't find its way to me.

But, even to this day, I use the magic candle at my parties. And it goes down very well. We light the candle, we blow it out and it lights up again. And what I usually do is take it out of the cake and hold it up, and say, 'Right, now let's sing "Happy Birthday".' And the children say, 'Oh, it's alight!' And I say, 'Where?' And I look at the child and say, 'You must have lit it. Would you blow it out, please?' So the child blows it out and I put it in the other hand, and the children are screaming because it's alight again, and we go on like this for about ten minutes, until I feel it's enough.

The children, these days, know the trick but they still enjoy my magic candle. It's amazing even though they know all about it, it's still a novelty. It's like Punch and Judy – they've seen it a hundred times but it's still exciting.

The cake cutting was always done by the child whose birthday it was and the ceremony was the final item on the tea-time agenda. And that was another social difference between the people who lived in central London and those who lived in the suburbs. With the top class of people, we used to cut the cake and distribute it to all the children. In the suburbs, and even today, you cut the cake and you put it in the party bag and they take it home. They don't eat it there. It's a stupid thing; they get a squashed piece of cake which they probably throw away. But children don't like cake today. They're fed up with cake; they've had so much of it.

There was an order to the cake cutting at my parties. We used to light the candles and have the magic candle ceremony and all sing 'Happy Birthday' to the child. When that was finished, the child would cut the cake and we'd all clap and cheer. Then we'd give the cake to the nanny to cut and pass around, and that was the ceremony of the cutting of the cake. But it could take a good ten or fifteen minutes just to do that.

Children's parties, today, usually last for about two hours, normally from 3.30 p.m. to 5.30 p.m. From 3.30 to 4.10, I used to play games with the children; I was very precise. I used to tell the parents, beforehand, exactly when we were going to have tea, so they'd be ready to move in. This was because, sometimes, you'd go to parties and they'd say, 'Give us another half-hour.' But you can't do it. You can only control children for a certain amount of time.

After 20 or 30 minutes at the tea table, I would return the children to the party room. In those days, I either did a film show or a magic show. Now, I don't show films at all. What with television and videos' that's all gone. So I just do magic.

Pat believes that children still enjoy films at parties, and so, in my heart of hearts, do I. But I think the parents would feel you were cheating them. I only used to put on Disney films for about 15 minutes, which the children loved. But I felt, with the videos coming on the market and all the television the children watched, that I was cheating the parents by not doing a live entertainment.

I built up a 40-minute magic show which I perform after tea, when the children are happy to sit down and watch. For my bag trick, I put four handkerchiefs in a bag. I ask four children to come up and I tell them to wave the handkerchiefs about. One by one, they put a handkerchief back in the bag and blow. Then I wave the bag about and say, 'Right, they're all gone,' and show the children. And, of course, the handkerchiefs haven't gone; they're still in the bag. And the children scream, 'No, they're not! They're still in there.' So, I try to do the trick a few more times, then I say to the birthday child, 'Well, I can't get it right. You put your hand in and take out the handkerchiefs for me.' He puts his hand in, and out comes a string of sausages!

Once, when the *Daily Mail* wrote a long article about me, they emphasised my magic act as 'Uncle Norman and Monty the Monkey'. Monty the Monkey is a puppet, and I included him much later on in my career. After that, I put the *Daily Mail* caption on my magic box, which is a large red box with my magic inside, and which I always bring along to parties now and keep in front of me.

When I bring out my magic box with the picture of Me and Monty the monkey on the front, the children are relaxed and ready to enjoy the show. I discovered, over the years, that a variety of entertainment works better than one or two types of amusement. After 30 minutes of magic, I finish off the act with Monty the Monkey and, possibly, Sandy the Squirrel or Peter the Penguin. This winds the party down and the children go home relaxed and happy, instead of excited.

I do the same sort of magic act each time because it goes down so well, but I vary it. I say, 'I've got a very bad memory and I've got to read in here what magic I'm going to do.' I open a book and a cut-out teddy bear pops up. The children shout, 'It's a teddy bear!' I say, 'What did you see?' They say it's a teddy bear and I say, 'Oh, you'd like to see it again?' I look down in the book, and up pops a rabbit. And they shout, 'It's a rabbit!' and I say, 'Well, make up your mind!' I do this two or three times, then I say, 'I'll tell you what we'll do: the boys all shout "rabbit" and the girls all shout "teddy bear" and when I open the book, you tell me who's right' And I say to the mothers, who are watching, 'You tell me who shouts the loudest,' because kids like to shout, which is good as long as it's controlled. Then I say, 'Ready, steady, go!' and the children shout 'rabbit!' and 'teddy bear!' And up pops a cut-out clown!

That lasts about five minutes. It's so simple, but it always goes down well. It's a good warm-up. And I involve the children in every part of my act. Then I have a magic egg trick, then a funnel trick where I involve the child's father. I make the child pour water in the father's pocket, then we pump him out by his arm like a village pump and it's hilarious. Even the parents love that. But you have to find an adult with a jacket on.

I did the trick at the Duke and Duchess of Kent's, one year. And there was no adult with a jacket on. The only person who had a jacket on was Prince Andrew. I knew him very well. I used to see him two or three times a week, sometimes, at parties. He must have been about seven years old at the time. So I said to him, 'Would you help me?' And he stood up, and I got Prince Edward and the birthday girl, Lady Helen Windsor, to help. I made Prince Andrew stand with his hands on his head. I got a funnel and put it in his pocket, and I got a glass of water and asked Lady Helen to pour it in his pocket I took it out and turned it upside down; there was no water in it. I never let anyone touch the pocket And everyone is wondering what we're going to do, so I talk to them about a village and I say we're going to make him into a village pump. I make the person put one arm like a spout and the other like a handle. That day, at the Duke and Duchess of Kent's, I got Prince Edward to hold Prince Andrew's hand and pump up and down when I told him to. And Lady Helen stood there with the glass. The idea was to get the water coming out of his pocket and up the arm and down.

I told the children to start pumping when I'd counted to three. Just as I counted to three, I said, 'Oh, I forgot, you're too small and the water might go on the carpet I'd better use the funnel to help you.' I did something to the funnel, then I counted to three and the children started pumping. And the water came out of Prince Andrew's sleeve and the children screamed with laughter. At the end, when there was no more water left, I asked Prince Andrew to put his hand in his pocket, and it was dry!

I found the two princes, Andrew and Edward, completely different in their personalities. Andrew was an extrovert, and Edward was a very quiet little boy.

There was more entertainment to follow. I used to do an additional trick, especially if there were boys. They always said, 'Ah, the water doesn't come out of the funnel, that's what it is!' And I'd

65

say, 'No?' And I'd get hold of the funnel, which was open, and I'd pour a couple of drops of water in it and over their heads, and they'd all scream. I'd say, 'See, the water goes right through, so it should have gone in the pocket'

I wasn't shown my magic tricks by one particular person. I just picked them up. But they're easy tricks, I'm not a magician. My grandchildren do card tricks that flabbergast me. I don't do any card tricks and I don't do any adult tricks, but I've got half a dozen tricks that I've picked up and that's enough. I vary my tricks in such a way that I can return to the same parties, year after year, and use my act again.

Because I always check the ages of the children at a party, I can be sure the presents I give out at the end will be appropriate. If they're seven-year-old boys, they'll all have swords, or something similar. And I give them high-quality stuff. And the girls have dolls and other toys.

The fashions in children's presents didn't change very much during the time I organised their parties, but they weren't always appreciated by those who were paying for them. At one stage, I was doing a party every year for the French bank, Credit Lyonnais. It was a Christmas party for about 200 children and we used to provide everything, including the food; but I used to have a friend, a special caterer, to do that because it was such a large affair – up to 30 or 40 children was enough for Pat. Anything over that, like a Christmas party, we'd call in the catering people.

At a Credit Lyonnais party, one Christmas, I gave the children small pistols. I was told off by the Belgian or French Managing Director. He said to me afterwards that he'd been disappointed; he didn't think guns were appropriate. I never gave out guns again. He was quite right about that. Guns had been fashionable presents for young boys in the 1950s but, by the 1970s, there was a new political correctness which affected many of the traditional gifts for children.

Another thing that's changed since I started giving parties, is that in the old days, Prince Andrew and Prince Edward and the others would say, 'Please can I sit on your lap, Mr Myers?' Both the boys and the girls wanted to come and sit on my lap. Today, you mustn't touch them. Not only mustn't they sit on your lap but you mustn't put your arm around them. That's the most terrible thing today about working with children. You dare not have any physical contact with them. But in the old days, up to about ten or twelve years ago, they used to sit on my lap and crowd around me. Now, it's very sad.

My diary for 1952 is full of names and addresses and telephone numbers of film operators. A typical page shows me organising children's parties, plus film projections for the Shell-Mex film library. As well as running their library, I used to send out projectionists to show their films. A page picked at random, Wednesday, 19 January 1952, reads: 'Shell Vintage MC, Harrow.' That's probably a motor cycle club. The names of the films shown at 8 p.m. were *Racing, Greece, Festival Log Book, Flight for Tomorrow* and *Mary Had a Little Lamb*; such was the variety of titles in the Shell-Mex library. And the clubs used to choose the titles themselves.

On the opposite page is an entry for a children's party. Here's a cowboy cartoon for a party in Prince of Wales Terrace, and another, on the twenty-second for a Mrs Cain, children's ages: three, four, five and six.

I was organising parties in 1997 and 1998, just before I retired, for parents of 50-something. And I'd say to them, 'You know, I used to do your parties.' And they'd say, 'What?' not realising how old I am.

Recently I organised a party for the daughter of a client I had also entertained as a young girl. Pat tells a lovely story. During the party, the grandmother of the birthday girl turned to her and said she used to have a Mr Myers to entertain the children at her own daughter's parties. 'Is this entertainer his son?' the grandmother wanted to know. And Pat had to tell her I was the very same person.

In fact, I never tell them my age. 'I'm only confessing it now because it's the end of my career, party-wise. Otherwise, I wouldn't tell people.

The Diplomat's Annual is a large, orange, A4 book; a thick hardback year book containing important anniversaries, month by month and country by country. There are sections for Heads of

States, National Flags, The Diplomatic Corps including the Representatives of the Nations of the British Commonwealth, and a list of The Representatives of Foreign States and Commonwealth Countries. It is a diplomat's handbook, containing everything a consulate person needs to get through the official year.

They used to ring me up and ask me to advertise in it. It's got every embassy in there. I used to advertise and get a lot of embassy parties. I did the Belgian Embassy's children's party for about ten years, the Venezuelan Embassy and others.

I also organised a number of parties in Scotland which took place at various country estates. The Duke of Buccleuch had a very large estate at Drumlarig Castle and I used to go up there to give parties. The chauffeur picked me up at the airport and I'd stay overnight and the Duchess used to take me back to the airport the next day. We had lovely parties there. The Duke had three or four estates but I also organised a party for him in London, with Prince Edward and the other royal children.

This happened in Edward Heath's Conservative government of the mid-seventies, when the unions were on strike and the nation's electricity supply was rationed to three days a week. I was doing a magic show, and, suddenly, all the lights went out. But they found candles and I was able to continue my act by candlelight.

The power-cut happened while I was entertaining at the Duke's London residence in Kensington, but I also learnt about the Duke's estates in the country. The story is told that when Scotland was divided into four quarters and dukedoms, the Duke of Buccleuch's ancestor was given land in the south. His estate stretched from Edinburgh in the east to west of Glasgow, an enormous area. And the present Duke still has the land.

I came to know the Duke quite well. He's a charming fellow, and his wife and children are delightful as well. Unfortunately, he had a hunting accident and he's confined to a wheelchair, but he gets around everywhere and all his estates are adapted areas for disabled people.

When I was in Scotland with my wife and some friends for a golfing holiday at Gleneagles, we drove past Bowhill, one of the homes of the Duke and Duchess of Buccleuch on the Scottish border. I suggested to Pat and our friends that, if the Duke and Duchess were in residence, they would be pleased to see us. They were at home and the Duchess invited us all to the top of the house, where we sat in the old nursery and had an informal tea. We chatted for an hour or so, and the visit was such a friendly one that it gave our holiday a wonderful start.

Another trip north was for the Countess of Seaford's children's party in Scotland. I flew up there on Saturday, and did the party at Cullen in Banffshire. The family had been kind enough to come 60 miles to meet me at Aberdeen airport. The party was for the Master of Seaford, now Viscount Reidhaven, who was aged five at the time.

Once again, I had to stay overnight in Aberdeen, but I had to dash back to London the next day to give a party in London at four o'clock on the Sunday afternoon for Lord Lever's children. There were no planes from Aberdeen to Edinburgh airport, so I hired a car and drove to Edinburgh very early in the morning, caught the plane down to London and arrived at Lord Lever's house in Eaton Square in time to do the party without any problems.

Although often pressed for time, I never felt tired or unable to perform the tasks I was engaged to do. I loved my work and the pleasure I got from entertaining the children carried me forward. When I got home, I probably said, 'That's it!' and relaxed, but whilst I was working it was like being on the stage, all the adrenalin was flowing.

My work could certainly be compared to that of an actor, preparing psychologically for a performance and experiencing 'butterflies' before beginning my act. To the end, I always got nervous before a party, in case it wasn't a success. But as soon as I saw the first child, I knew it was going to work.

I thought about my work constantly. As soon as one party was over, the next one was uppermost in my mind. I was planning and working things out and making notes all the time. I had to make sure everything was working. My career was built on a range of skills: organisation, application, love for my work, my ability to capitalise on a lucky break, and, to put it in two words, me personally.

It had to be me. People liked me when they saw me and we got on very well together, and they repeated the exercise, that was the point. When I organised parties for one family, my reputation spread throughout the family and their connections. Take the Londonderry family, The Marquis of Londonderry's sister was Lady Annabel Birley, or Lady Annabel Goldsmith as she is now. When she was Lady Annabel Birley, she had several children and I organised the parties for her elder boys, back in the mid-sixties. The first party was at the Clermont Club, which belonged to John Aspinall and was a favourite haunt of the 'infamous' Lord Lucan. The following year, Lady Annabel combined a party with her brother, the Marquess, at the De Vere Hotel in Kensington. Then, when she was married to Sir James Goldsmith, she had three more children and I did all their parties, year after year.

And the Marquess of Londonderry: I organised all his children's parties. He lived near Lady Annabel, on Richmond Green, and had two sons, Frederick, now Lord Castlereagh, and Reginald. From 1980 until 1985, I did their parties, twice a year.

Lady Annabel is now the widow of the late Sir James Goldsmith. She divorced Mark Birley, who owned Annabel's, the famous nightclub he named after her, and married Sir James Goldsmith and lived in Ormley Lodge. That used to belong to the Howard de Waldens until Sir James bought it. They had three children: Zac, who's just got married to Vivien Ventura's child. I did her parties, as well. And, of course, there's Jemima, who's married to the cricketer, Imran Khan. In 1999 I organised a summer party for the Goldsmiths at Ormley Lodge with Jemima's little boy, Sulieman, who is now nearly four years old.

Another of the Londonderrys, Lady Annabel's sister, Lady Jane, was maid of honour at the Queen's coronation and married Max, Lord Rayne. The Raynes had four children and I did all their parties. They lived in a wonderful house in Hampstead and I went there several times a year, for many years. I started with Natasha as a two-year-old in 1968, then came Nicholas, three years old in 1972, Tamara, who was four in 1974, right through to Alexander in 1980 and finishing in 1983. That's why I kept a filing system;

why I cross-referenced everything. I used to organise parties for whole families for years and years without repeating myself.

And so I was asked, again and again, to town houses and country estates. The children didn't say, 'Oh God, it's him again!' because they never saw the same thing twice. The Brady Boys' Club in Whitechapel, the springboard for my facility with organisation and entertainment, had propelled me to the highest level. I had travelled a long way from my roots but those youthful experiences were my capital and my good fortune. They had made me feel confident in my ability to organise and at ease with the people I met.

I got a call, one day, from a Mrs Phillips. She said, 'Natasha saw you at a friend's party and she'd like you to do her party.' I didn't know the Phillips family, at all. It was in the country, round about Oxfordshire. I had organised a dozen parties in that area: Wantage and all around there, the racing area, East Hendred, for the Hendersons, the Astors, and many other people.

I drove up to the Phillips's with my son, Geoffrey. I was shown the rooms in which they were having the party and when I glanced at the table plan, I saw it said Prince Edward and Prince Andrew and all the children of the top families. I found out, in time, that Mrs Phillips was the daughter of Lady Zia Wernher, who was a best friend of the Queen and Prince Philip. The Queen and the Duke of Edinburgh always spent their wedding anniversary at, Luton Hoo, the ancestral home of Lady Zia Werhner, the mother of Mrs Phillips, so all the royal children were there.

I did not need to consult *Debrett's* for my dealings with the aristocracy. But, strangely enough, I used to get *Who's Who*, free, for my cross-referencing because the publishers were Adam Black. Adam Black's wife is the daughter of Lady Lowson and I used to write to him every three or four years and he'd let me have a copy.

Lady Lowson, as I have mentioned, was the wife of the Lord Mayor of London and was one of the first to give a children's party I organised. With Lady Lowson and her son-in-law, the Earl of Kinnoull, who had three or four children, and the Blacks, I used to go around the families and do all their parties. The Earl of Kinnoull was the seventeenth earl. He was a charming fellow and we were on first-name terms and very great friends.

When I received a telephone call for a party, I could consult my cross-referenced filing system and check the connections. For instance, Geoffrey Robinson, the ex-Paymaster General who lent a large sum of money to Peter Mandelson, so the minister could purchase a luxury house. I did many parties for Geoffrey Robinson, especially at his magnificent estate near Godalming in Surrey. Pat and I, and our helpers, would arrive early in the afternoon with all the party food and other equipment. There was only a maid there, and she would let us in. We knew our way around and went straight to the large kitchen, where Pat and her helpers prepared the tea. Meanwhile, I went into the sitting room and the garden and set up the entertainment and laid the table for tea. When the children arrived I'd greet them and play games with them for an hour or so, then we'd sit down to tea, after which I'd provide the entertainment.

In the early days, we had films and a magic show; in later years, we organised a top-class magician from the Inner Magic Circle. Each year, we would provide a different birthday cake: one year, it was in the shape of a racing car; in other years, we had a fort, a monster and a space rocket We organised the parties for his two children from 1979 to 1990, when Alexander turned 13. I especially enjoyed giving the children their 'going home' presents and, afterwards, sitting down with Geoffrey Robinson and having a drink and a talk.

Another client was the Earl of Radnor, who has an estate, Longford Castle, near Salisbury in Wiltshire, which is two miles south of Salisbury on the Ringwood road. You'd pass it, and you wouldn't even know it was there because there's a big wall along the road. But, when you go inside, there's the most amazing castle, just like the Tower of London. And the whole family live there; his second wife had four daughters and I did their parties. His son, who'd grown up and whose parties I didn't organise, married Lord Gilmour's daughter. Lord Gilmour's wife is the sister of the Duke of Buccleuch. Everybody's connected with everybody else and I go all round the families.

I organised the children's parties for the Gilmours at Ferry Lodge, an addition to the Duke of Northumberland's Syon House. Lady Gilmour was the Duke's aunt, and the Duke also owned Alnwick Castle in Northumberland. The Dowager Duchess of Buccleuch was the mother of Lady Gilmour and the Duke of Buccleuch, and their aunt is H.R.H. Princess Alice Dowager Duchess of Gloucester, who's nearly the same age as the Queen Mother.

The Dowager Duchess of Buccleuch was also almost the same age as the Queen Mother, as well. I used to sit with her, and we used to have long conversations. I'm not sure if she's still alive but I used to talk to her about all that crowd, because H.R.H. Princess Alice of Gloucester and the Queen Mother and the Duchess of Buccleuch were all contemporaries. We used to have wonderful conversations. I won't repeat them, but they were wonderful!

I always got on well with my clients and enjoyed many conversations with titled people, young and old. When I went up to the Ogilvys at Airlie Castle in Scotland, I had tea with the Dowager Countess of Airlie, who was also in the same age group as the Queen Mother. We'd sit and chat like old friends and Pat used to come with me.

It was one of the three Ogilvy brothers, Angus, who married Princess Alexandra, the Queen's cousin. All these people were completely unaffected. They were so friendly, and so nice and so normal. They had nothing to sell or prove to anyone; they could simply relax and enjoy a conversation.

On one occasion, I was driving past Buckingham Palace on my way to Hyde Park Corner. I was going round the Queen Victoria Memorial when I was stopped by a policeman, holding up the traffic. A car glided out of the Palace and, as it slowed down in front of me, two little boys leaned out of the window and shouted excitedly, 'Look, it's Mr Myers! Hullo, Mr Myers!' It was Prince Edward and James Ogilvy. They'd seen me twice that week at friends' parties and they were thrilled to see me again, like that.

The Tennants were another titled family I came to know through my work. Mr Colin and Lady Anne Tennant, now Lord and Lady Glenconner, had a house in Tite Street in the sixties. In the dining room there, they had about eight Francis Bacon paintings. They were magnificent.

But that's a very sad family, now. Lady Anne was the daughter of the Earl of Leicester and she was, or is, lady-in-waiting to Princess Margaret. It was Colin Tennant who bought the island of Mustique and gave some land to Princess Margaret on which she built a house. Princess Margaret recently gave the house to her son, Viscount Linley, and he sold it.

The Tennants had five children: three boys and twin girls and I used to do all their parties. Funnily enough, Colin Tennant's eldest son, Charles, went to boarding school with my son, Geoffrey, in Sussex. I remember, we used to meet Lady Anne on the railway station, going back to school, as well as at parties. Unfortunately, Charles died young. The bright side to the family story is the twin daughters, who are very happy.

Another family I came to know was the Dudleys – Earl and Countess of Dudley. The Countess was formerly the American actress Maureen Swanson. They lived in Kensington and had five girls and a boy, and they were charming people. And living opposite them were the Tates and I used to do their parties, as well. They have five boys and a girl too!

In 1966, I found myself in Scotland again, as I regularly did, this time to organise a party for Lord and Lady Rotherwick in Kilmarnock. Lord Rotherwick's family name is Cayzer and I'd done some parties for his brother, who had three daughters, in Ilchester Place, just by Holland Park. And I've recently given parties for the children of the three daughters, so I've done the second generation of the Cayzers.

I've also done a party for Robin, one of Lord Rotherwick's children who's married and had children. Lord Rotherwick bought the estate next to the Duke of Malborough's estate at Blenheim, and one year, I organised a Christmas party for the estate workers at Blenheim Palace. I'd already been round there as a visitor, and it was very impressive.

The Cayzer girls all went to Lady Eden School, the famous girls' school in Victoria Road, Kensington. Lady Eden was a very English school whereas Hill House, where a lot of the boys went, had a large number of foreign diplomats' children. At one stage, I was doing so many parties for the children at Lady Eden, I couldn't go past the school without the children shouting, 'Hallo, Mr Myers!'

Another estate workers' children's party I was asked to do was Lord Vestey's. He's a great friend of Prince Charles. I did his Christmas parties for several years. He had an enormous property at Stowell Park in Oxfordshire, near Highgrove, where Prince Charles lives. Prince Charles bought his house from Maurice Macmillan, Harold Macmillan's son, who died before his father.

I used to entertain at parties for the Faber family, as well. Mrs Faber, who lived in Chester Square, SW1, was the eldest daughter of Harold Macmillan, the Prime Minister before Harold Wilson. Their eldest son, David, became an MP then married, divorced and married again. He was a great friend of David Linley, and I remember both Davids, Faber and Linley, hiding under the tea table during David Faber's parties.

Apart from the strange episode of Candid Camera's Jonathan Routh wanting a Punch and Judy show in bed, there was a further unusual request I received for a puppet show. We were once asked to do a Punch and Judy show for a twenty-first birthday party held at Les Ambassadeurs in Hamilton Place, where I had organised many parties for the family of John Mills, the owner of the club. I can't remember the name of the people whose party it was, but we did it through the Mills family. After Annabel's, 'Les A' was the top place to go.

Once again, Vic and I went along, with our equipment. This time, it was a glorious summer's day and the party was out on the club terrace, in the open. We put a Punch and Judy show on for these grown-ups and they had a wonderful time; they thoroughly enjoyed it. We didn't adapt the show to make it more in line with adult taste, as some people might have done. We did the traditional children's Punch and Judy show for a twenty-first birthday party, and they loved it Usually, I found Punch and Judy was very popular with children up to the age of about six. After that, they get a bit blasé.

John Mills, the casino and nightclub owner, was the proprietor of Les Ambassadeurs in Hamilton Place, Park Lane, and his sister is an Italian countess (as is Sir Charles Forte's daughter, whose children's parties I also organised). Pat and I became such good friends with the daughter of the owners of Les Ambassadeurs, that, for our twenty-fifth wedding anniversary in 1972, the Italian countess, Carole Nardi-Die, invited us to dine at Les Ambassadeurs, on the house, where we enjoyed a gargantuan meal and in those days, I used to enjoy brandy and a big cigar afterwards! We dined with the owner's mother and, afterwards, were taken up to her apartment, above the club.

Pat was more than the catering corps in my organisation. At a moment's notice, she could become a star entertainer. Her 'Tommy Cooper act' was much appreciated in the 1970s. Tommy Cooper was a comedian who mixed up his magic in such a way that everybody thought he couldn't do any tricks. I'll let Pat take over the story: 'One day, Norman's magician let him down and he didn't know what to do, so he asked me to go along, instead. I can't remember the name of the client; a pop star I think he was. When I got to the door, the chap's face dropped. "Oh," he said, "I was expecting a man." I said, "I'm sorry, but he's been taken ill and I'm taking over for today." He asked, "Can you do magic?" and I said, "Of course I can." He had dozens of platinum discs in his living room.

"I played party games with the children first, as usual, then it came to doing the magic. Norman had shown me a few tricks beforehand, roughly. So I said to the birthday boy, "Come on, you can come and help me." And I put on the show, and he helped, then I deliberately let the tricks go wrong. I said to the boy, "You can help me out with this,' and, by this time, the children were all in hysterics. When I got home, I said to Norman, "Oh, it went all right,' and that was it, I thought. The next day, the mother phoned and asked to speak to me. She told me: "I just want to say thank you so much, you were brilliant!"'

In the mid-1980s, I discovered I had heart trouble and went into hospital for a by-pass operation. Naturally, Pat was there to help me with my business commitments. For many years, I used to do a Christmas party for Lord Astor, down at Hever Castle in Kent. It was a private party, for his family. Of course, I couldn't go just after my surgery, and I was panicking; I didn't want to cancel it. So I sent Vic down to Hever, and I also sent Pat. I gave Pat some magic to do and they managed the party completely successfully.

Since my illness, Pat has always gone to the children's parties with me. Especially these days when they're so fussy about leaving children with men. If the children want to hold hands with an adult, they can do so with her and everything's fine. If a child is shy and clinging to her mother, it's no problem for her to go up to the child and say, 'Come on, you can join in the games with me.' The child will go with her because she's a woman. The child can sit on Pat's lap, but not on mine.

We've been married now for over fifty-two years, and have a successful working partnership, as well as a domestic one. We complement each other and support each other, although Pat accuses me of organising her and being a bully!

When I organised parties in Scotland, I often had to stay overnight. Sometimes, I would visit the famous golf course at Gleneagles. The Gleneagles Hotel was expensive, but, on the golf course below, they had a club. In the club, they had a restaurant, and a huge, luxury double suite of rooms. I discovered this one year, and they let me stay there and only charged about 14 guineas a time. So we stayed there for several years in succession. We used to take friends up there because it was a double suite. I used to play golf there and it was wonderful.

About a year ago, I found a letter from the management at Gleneagles, dated 1971, saying how they were looking forward to seeing me this year, as every year, and the prices were still only 14 guineas a night. I wrote back to the present management saying I was in receipt of their letter – I put the date but omitted the year – and would be delighted to come again this year and I presumed the rooms were still 14 guineas a night. But instead of getting a humorous letter back, I got the most stupid formal letter, saying, 'Dear Mr Myers, you realise, of course, prices have risen ...' So there you are, that's Gleneagles. No sense of humour, whatsoever.

6

Friends in High Places

Out of interest, in the mid-1960s, I decided to compile a list of my clients who were known to the general public in one sphere or another. This VIP list, which I have kept, includes clients for whom I organised parties from January 1950 to August 1998. There are kings and princesses and Saudi royal family, titled families and film stars, Greek shipping magnates and pop stars, charity organisations, politicians and business tycoons.

About a month before a child's birthday I would send a postcard to the parents, with my name, address and telephone number on the card and write, 'As you may remember, we have had the pleasure in the past of supplying the entertainment at your annual children's party. Should you be holding a party this year, we shall be only too pleased to be of assistance in the matter. Norman Myers'.

Beneath the reminder, the card said: 'Mr Norman Myers takes complete charge of parties on request and can provide games and competitions, film shows, Punch and Judy shows, magic and ventriloquism, puppets, presents, catering and mini disco.' This broad range of party activities gave party holders everything they needed.

Even now, in my eightieth year, I am still busy entertaining children, but I no longer advertise, so I assume the phone calls keep coming through personal recommendation. Or they're reading an old magazine. I never ask where they've got my name from. I don't want to know; there's no point.

Among my photographs and memorabilia is a framed certificate of my Freedom of the City of London. You have to be proposed and seconded by a councillor in the City. Then, if they think you're suitable, they elect you as a Freeman of the City of London. The advantage you have is that you can drive your sheep across London Bridge – although I've yet to exercise this right.

After receiving my Freedom of the City, I went on to join the Guild of Freemen. We have meetings in the City and we have a banquet in the Guildhall, once a year. It's a very pleasant pastime and we have extremely interesting people as guests of honour. You have seven or eight hundred people in the Guildhall and it's magnificent.

I'm also a member of the Royal Enclosure at Ascot because the Clerk of the Course was a client of mine. I said to him, one day, that I'd like to go and he said, 'I'll recommend you.' He proposed me, and Pat and I have been going for about 20 years now. I wear my grey morning suit and top hat and we have a marvellous picnic in the reserved part. We used to go on Ladies' Day but we found it was too crowded, so we usually go on the Wednesday and it's very pleasant.

Another communication which hangs, framed, in my bathroom is a letter from the Queen saying she is sorry that Pat and I cannot attend her garden party. The Queen has garden parties every year but, in 1997, she had her Golden Wedding. She asked anyone who had a Golden Wedding, during that particular period, to write in and, if there were places available, you'd be invited to the Palace Garden Party to celebrate her Golden Wedding, and yours. Unfortunately, there were about 40,000 or 50,000 people celebrating their Golden Wedding at the same time. Nobody thought there'd be that many. They could only invite about 4,000 people so the ones who couldn't go received that letter from the Queen. But the following year, we were invited.

It's an enormous garden and you go through the Palace and it's quite a pleasant occasion. It's very formal and I wore my morning suit and top hat. Halfway through the proceedings, everybody forms two lines and half the Royals go in one direction and half of them in the other. It's decided beforehand which people will be pointed out to them and they stop and talk for two minutes to each of them. Although I have met many of the country's top families, I have yet to meet the Queen and Prince Phillip or Prince Charles. But I did a party, about two years ago, and the PR person who organised it is now the Countess of Wessex, Prince Edward's wife. They had a polo match, up at Cirencester Park, and a firm called Thomas Goode who are at the top end of china and porcelain manufacturing, sponsored it. They rang me up and said, as there were going to be a lot of children there, would I organise the children while the polo match was on and they were having lunch.

When I arrived at the polo match, there must have been about 200 people, but very few children. I expected to find 20 or 30 children so I could entertain them with my games and magic while the event was going on. I finished up with three children; hardly anyone had brought their children with them – they seemed to be enjoying themselves without them. But, whilst the polo match was going on and I was entertaining the three children, Tiggy Legge Bourke was standing there with Prince William and Prince Harry, watching their father playing polo. There was a write-up about the match in *Harpers and Queen*. I've got a copy of it somewhere.

I've known the former royal nanny, Tiggy Legge Bourke, for many years. She had a nursery school and started doing parties herself. But being connected with everyone, she rang me up and gave me her parties. Princess Diana was at the parties with her sons, when they were very small. The first time I saw Prince Harry was when he was only three years old, at his nursery school in Notting Hill.

I do a little game of 'Pass the Parcel' in which there's a present. But I never know whether a boy or a girl is going to get it and it might be the wrong present. I remember Prince Harry getting the parcel, and he got a ring. I said to him, 'Give it back to me and I'll get you a boy's present.' 'Oh no,' he said. He wanted the ring and he kept it.

For many years, it was the so-called 'nanny mafia' who brought so much business to me. The Royals had three nannies: Mabel for Prince Edward and Prince Andrew, there was Princess Margaret's nanny, who was an older nanny, and the Duchess of Kent's nanny, and I used to meet them quite a lot. But the doyenne of the nannies was Lord Airlie's nanny, Nanny Ellis, who wasn't the most important nanny but everyone looked up to her. We became very good friends from about 1962, onwards. She's about 70 now, so I imagine she was about 30 or 40 years old then.

The nannies of the late twentieth are very different from the nannies of the mid-1900s. The Norland nannies are quite young. The Norland Agency, in Holland Park, is the top organisation and, these days, if you want to be a real nanny you have to go through the Norland school. It's the establishment's agency, and it's been going for many years. But, in the period I'm talking about, the nannies either used to be very young or, by the time I knew them, they were mature women. These older women had usually started working for a family when they were quite young, and had stayed with the one family all the time.

Lord Ogilvy, who became the Earl of Airlie when his father died, was the father of six children and I organised the children's parties for him, year after year. I knew his nannies very well, and all the nannies who came to the parties. Before Lord Ogilvy became the Earl, the family lived in St Leonard's Terrace in Chelsea. One day, their nanny, Nanny Ellis, wanted to give a nannies' party and Lord Ogilvy said she could hold it in his home. Of course, Nanny Ellis got in touch with me and asked me to organise it. We held the party at the top of the house, on the fourth floor where the children's nursery is, and I organised a good film for them. When I asked about numbers, Lord Ogilvy's nanny told me she'd invited about 30 nannies. But, as I was to find out, this was not the case.

They were the real nannies, of the old school. They don't make them like that any more. And I thought to myself, as I knew them all and I knew the situation, I'd give them a little present to go home with, just as their charges were given one when they went home. So Pat and I went out and bought 30 quarter-pound boxes of Dairy Milk chocolates, wrapped them nicely and put them in a bag, and took them to the nannies' party. When the nannies arrived, Nanny Ellis received them with Lord Ogilvy and he took them into the sitting room where they had sherry and biscuits.

Then they all went upstairs, where my operator was waiting to show them a film.

While the nannies enjoyed their film, I sat downstairs, talking and having a drink with Lord Ogilvy. I went upstairs, just before the film finished, and checked that everything had gone well. The nannies were delighted with everything and were thanking Nanny Ellis and getting ready to go home. I had already mentioned the presents I'd brought, but I suddenly found myself with a dilemma. Some nannies who hadn't been invited had turned up. So, instead of 30 nannies, there were 33 nannies. And I only had 30 presents. I wondered what I could do.

The first nanny departed and we said goodbye to her. The second nanny went and we said goodbye; the third nanny left, we said goodbye. Then we started giving out the presents. So far, so good. Within five minutes, the first three nannies came running back. They'd met the other nannies outside. 'We haven't had our presents,' they said, just like the children! I was lucky: the three royal nannies didn't mind not having a present, and we gave them to the other nannies.

Nanny Ellis retired many years later, when the youngest Ogilvy had gone off to boarding school. Lord Airlie, as Lord Ogilvy had now become, had a grace and favour house in St James's Palace, because he was Lord Chamberlain to the Queen. He gave another party for Nanny Ellis, as a retirement party, at St James's Palace and told her she could invite all her friends who were ex-nannies. The only two people who were invited who were not ex-nannies were Pat and me. It was quite an honour.

It was a wonderful party, and all the old nannies were there and a lot of them came up and said, 'Mr Myers, how lovely to see you. I'm Nanny Ilchester; I'm Nanny So-and-so.' They named themselves after the family they'd worked for. Unfortunately, I think there are only one or two of them left, now. It's very sad. Yesterday's generation has gone, and it's never going to come back.

For the last ten years, nannies have no longer been nannies; they're either au pairs or very young Norland girls. I'm not denigrating them; they're efficient people, but as far as I'm concerned, they haven't got that warmth. They're not like the old nannies and they change jobs quite a lot. A lot of the old nannies came from Scotland and and were often crofters' children. The Queen's nannies, most of them, came from north of the border, or they were country girls who joined the family locally.

The style of nanny started to change in the early seventies. The old tribe has nearly disappeared. I call them the 'nanny mafia' because, in some respects, they were very influential people. What they said, went, as regards the children. I saw at first-hand the social life of the old-style nanny. When the children had parties, it was the nannies' great pleasure to organise tea for their nanny-friends. Not only did they all know each other from taking the children to and from school but they met each other, walking in Kensington Park.

Although I regret not having organised parties at Buckingham Palace itself, I had the pleasure of being closely associated with the Royal Family through the Duke and Duchess of Kent and the Duke and Duchess of Gloucester. I always used to take Vic along with me to their parties. We gave them Punch and Judy and magic and games – the lot. I also knew King Constantine of Greece and I have a picture in my sitting room of the King and me together.

I used to do the parties for most of the Greek shipping million-aires who lived in London, and once you did a party for one of them, you did parties for the lot. There were about ten families called Lemos, all relatives. They were tycoons, like Onassis and Niarchos. Livanos is another Greek shipping tycoon on the list of top people for whom I have organised a great number of parties. Livanos's wife was originally married to the Duke of Marlborough, and there was a lot of tragedy in that family. Goulandris was another well-known Greek name I was asked to do parties for. Lykiadopolous is another Greek magnate whose home I knew well. The shipping millionaires maintained London homes and lived there for the tax advantages. They either had big houses in Bishops Avenue, which is the millionaires' row in London, or houses in Chelsea or Kensington, or, more usually, enormous apartments in Grosvenor Square, with staff and exquisite paintings.

Some of the Greeks, like Niarchos, who was connected with Onassis, I only did their parties once. The Goulandris family, the Lemoses and the Nomekos family, I organised parties for several times. The Nomekos family were great friends of King Constantine and recommended me for the King's party.

As well as doing a children's party for King Constantine, I organised a party for him when he invited the students he had studied with in Greece to visit him. I had my professional photographer there and he took some wonderful shots of the party, including the one I have of me with the King.

I used to do a lot of parties at the Hellenic College, just off Sloane Street. It's the school where most of the Greeks send their children, and I used to meet the King's daughter there. The college hired out its premises to school parents who wanted to hold parties there, and I used to organise them about once a week.

Once I had organised a party for one family in a network of families, I was immediately recommended to the others. I did one or two banks, as well, but mainly the Credit Lyonnais. Having done it once, I organised their parties for about ten years. That was a very, very big party.

In addition I used to give parties for the Saudi Royal Family. They would come to England in the summer, to get away from the heat of the Gulf, and they all had estates in London and further out, such as at Windsor. I did one party – the estate was somewhere in the Berkshire countryside and was completely surrounded by walls and security. It was the height of summer, in June, and the family, about six or seven children and lots of women, wanted a firework party. Being me, I couldn't say 'No'. I said, 'Yes, no problem,' and I got in touch with the right people and said, 'Look, I've got to do this party in daytime, in June; can you help?'

A firework expert arrived and spent a long time fixing up the display in the grounds. Then, at the appropriate moment, the fireworks began spectacularly, with a really special display for broad daylight And I think I charged about £4,000 just for 12 or 15 minutes' worth of fireworks. Price was no object.

One day, I thought I was free to sneak in an afternoon's golf at my club and, by 5 p.m., I had reached the eighth tee, the one

85

furthest from the clubhouse. Then I looked up to see the club professional running towards me. Pat had rung the club with the
message that a Saudi Prince wanted me to organise a party for his
son in one hour's time. I ran back to the clubhouse, changed,
rushed home for my party gear, and was at the Prince's house in
Holland Park at 6 p.m.. The party went on until 10 p.m. that night.

My services for a recent Saudi party at the Hilton, however,
were soundly rejected. Vic and I were booked to do a Punch and
Judy show for the occasion. At the last minute, the organisers cancelled. It was a party for Saudi women and Vic and I, whether hid-
den behind a puppet theatre or not, were considered too much of a
threat to the women's virtue. The management wanted a 'female'
Punch and Judy show. And Vic was the wrong shape!

The main postal areas in which I worked were SW1, SW3, SW5
and SW7, and W1 and W8. These addresses are where the top
people lived in London. In the sixties and seventies, most of the
top people lived south of Hyde Park. If you lived to the north of
Hyde Park, it wasn't quite the thing. Everybody lived in Chelsea
and Knightsbridge and Kensington. When prices rose, in the mid-
1980s, the next generation couldn't afford to buy those houses, so
they crossed the bridges to Battersea and Clapham and these areas
became gentrified and up-market.

For £150,000 to £250,000 in those days, you could buy the
most fabulous houses south of the river, whereas those same
houses, in Chelsea, would cost you £750,000 to £800,000. Today,
those houses in Battersea are worth three-quarters of a million,
and the houses in Chelsea are worth two or three million. That's
the way property's gone and that's the way people have moved.

But, then, everybody lived north of the river but south of the
park, in Chelsea and Kensington. Notting Hill and Bayswater
weren't done but, gradually, they became acceptable. Ladbroke
Grove went upmarket and that's how it all grew. Towards the end
of my career, I found I was doing a lot of parties in Battersea
and Clapham and Wandsworth. They might not have been titled
people, but they were landed people, the gentry.

There were parties for Lady Brooke, who was married to the

son of the Earl of Warwick, 1963 twice, 1964 twice. Charlotte was 21 in 1979 and Guy got married in 1982, to Suzy Coggald, in Australia. The Earl sold all his possessions, and he sold his castle to Madame Tussaud's, who still own it. The family lived in a small house opposite Hyde Park, near the Albert Hall. I used to do all their parties there. The young Lord Brooke is now the Earl of Warwick; his father died.

Lady Farnham was another recipient of my entertainment services. Lord and Lady Farnham were a charming couple, who lived in a small house in Chelsea. Lord Farnham is the Assistant Grand Master of the English Masons; he's one of the top Freemasons in the country. And The Cardross family, we were great friends with; they lived off Tregunter Road in Earl's Court.

Another name in my files is Lady Gordon-Lennox. She is the Duke of Richmond and Gordon's daughter-in-law. Her husband, Nicholas Gordon-Lennox, is a member of the diplomatic corps and was the British Ambassador in Spain for a long time. The Duke of Richmond and Gordon owns Goodwood, where they have the racing. And Lady Freyberg – her father-in-law was a VC, I believe. They had a beautiful house in the country, either Surrey or Sussex, and I used to do a lot of parties there. I think the original family came from Australia or New Zealand.

Another great friend was the Marchioness of Bute. The Marquess and Marchioness of Bute lived in Chelsea Square, and I did dozens and dozens of parties for them there. They also lived in Scotland, where we had lunch with them and they put us up for the night. In 1965 Sophie was nine years old, John was seven – John is now the Marquess – and Anthony was four.

Lord and Lady Birdwood were the most charming people. They lived in a small house at the back of Royal Hospital Road and their daughter was called Sophie. They were very friendly with the chap who plays vampires in the films, Christopher Lee. Sophie and Christopher Lee's daughter went to the same school and were very great friends.

We used to do a lot of parties, week after week, at the Brompton Oratory. It had a beautiful big hall and we did hundreds of parties there because most of the Kensington and Chelsea set used to book it. Lady Dudley used to have parties there, I remember. We used to organise parties for 60 children there, and provide the food, as well.

I once did a party for Sophie Birdwood at the Brompton Oratory and, on the morning of the party, Lady Birdwood rang up and said she was terribly sorry but Sophie was very ill. She had flu or something, and was in bed and couldn't go to the party. In order not to disappoint the other children, Lady Birdwood decided to continue the party with Christopher Lee's daughter, Christina, as the hostess. So I arrived at the Brompton Oratory and did the party. Everyone was there, except poor Sophie. But, at the end of the party, I went back to the Birdwoods' house and gave Sophie a very nice present, because I was sorry that she wasn't at her own party.

Lady Napier and Ettrick was another client. Her husband was a courtier to Prince Philip, I think. And Lady Astor was a regular client. There were about six Astors, and I used to do all their parties. There was Lord Astor at Hever, another up in Oxford; Gavin Astor owned *The Times* and I used to do his parties. I went from one to the other and organised their parties for years.

Looking back, over all the parties I've given and all the children I've met, I cannot think of a child who behaved badly. They were an absolute pleasure to do parties for. They were just normal boys and girls. I won't say they were goody-goodies but they were a pleasure to be with. Possibly the reason the children were well-behaved was because the nannies, in those days, were very firm. Recently, in the last ten years, one notices the children are more spoilt, less supervised. Also, the whole attitude to parties has changed. With so many things going on today, like football parties and ten-pin bowling parties or video parties, the ordinary, basic children's party is dying out.

Plus the fact, and this is a point I've got to raise, there are so many entertainers on the scene who are not entertainers but think they are, that people hire them once and say, 'If this is the standard of entertainment, we won't have this again'. So they take the children out, or have a few of them in, or they go to McDonald's, and that's what's happening now.

When I've done parties in the last couple of years and people have just picked my name from somewhere, I have to say, with or without shooting a line, that they soon realise the difference between a party and a party. They've never seen anything like how we handle the children, how they behave and enjoy themselves. Often, the children go wild with these other people. I'm not saying all of them, but some of them. Most of them simply excite the children. They're people whose names I won't mention. But the parents don't like it and won't repeat the exercise.

Lady Ednam, later Lady Dudley, the former Maureen Swanson, was very elegant and beautiful and friendly, a charming person. The first party I did for them, the child was only one year old. They had a family party in the country but, after that, they came to Kensington and, as I said, they had five girls and a boy and I did most of their parties. They lived at the back of Lady Eden School, in Eldon Road, at the back of Barker's and Kensington High Street.

Lady Aberdare is another name in my files, as is Lady St Just. Her daughter was very friendly with David Linley. They used to invite him to their parties. The last party I remember doing there was when the children were growing up; they were about nine or ten. At that age, I used to organise acting parties.

You sit the children down and you give them a text to read. It's a melodrama, usually, with the villain, the hero and the simple maid and her animals. You have four children reading the script, and whoever the other children enjoy listening to most, they clap the loudest. And one becomes the hero, one becomes the heroine, and so on. And then we put the play on; it takes about two minutes, but I've got all the details written down. It's a wonderful game and you can play it with adults. I've done it on New Year's Eve with friends. And David, Viscount Linley, was very good at it. He was a shy boy, but he used to blossom in this sort of play.

I organised a lot of parties at San Lorenzo in Beauchamp Place, Knightsbridge, the famous restaurant owned by the Berni family.

They had another San Lorenzo, down in Wimbledon. Because they were so busy during the week, I used to do their children's parties on a Sunday, in Wimbledon. I organised parties for Prince Loewenstein, Mick Jagger's financial adviser, and through him, I did Mick Jagger's, and through Mick Jagger I did the Bernis' and that's how bookings grew.

In fact, on our fortieth wedding anniversary, I rang up the Bernis, because you can never get in their restaurant at Beauchamp Place, and asked if there was a possibility of a table and they said, 'Sorry, we're solidly booked up.' So I said, I don't know if you remember me, and I told him who I was, and they fitted me in! I didn't recognise anybody, but Princess Diana might have been there; she often was. But it was wonderful, going there, and all because of the connection.

Princess Essim Jah doesn't have a surname that is immediately recognisable, but it is the family name of the man who was the richest person in the world the Nizam of Hyderabad. At one stage, he was famous for all the jewels he possessed. He ended up living in a house in London, next door to the former Liberal Party leader, Jeremy Thorpe. I did a party for Jeremy Thorpe's son at Lambeth Palace; his mother organised it. And that's how I went from one party to another, everything was interconnected.

A good example of this interconnection was when President Kennedy's press secretary, Pierre Salinger, came over to England. I did his children's party. I also organised parties for a number of children of American movie producers and directors. Harry Saltzman, the producer of the James Bond films, was a client of mine for many years. He used to have his parties at the Dorchester, and invite the current James Bond to attend. It was quite a thrill. We had Sean Connery there and George Lazenby and whoever was Bond at the time. I've played golf behind Sean Connery at Gleneagles, so I have met him. He was a charming chap, and, in those days, he had a lot of hair.

But for me, Sam Spiegel was the epitome of an American film producer. He was the number one producer in America, natural successor to Sam Goldwyn. He walked about with an entourage, and he had a permanent suite in the Grosvenor House, Park Lane. That's where he lived when he was in London. He had a young son in London. The boy went to one of the schools in Hampstead and he used to invite his friends to his parties – and I did all the parties. Sam Spiegel was not a big man. He was a tiny, tubby fellow, but the aura around him was about ten feet tall. He was an amazing chap.

Stanley Donen was another film producer whose parties I regularly organised. He lived in Chester Square, I think. Unlike the titled families, there was no network of film directors and producers to recommend my services around town, but the children of these movie moguls usually attended the same schools. Probably, the children went to Hill House or Wetherby's or to the school of a particular area, then the nannies or mothers would ask me to come.

Another personality who called on me for his children's parties was the food columnist, Quentin Crewe. He was in a wheelchair, and had been a cripple from birth. The interesting thing was, I did one of my many parties for Lord Airlie in St Leonard's Terrace, Chelsea, on a Monday or a Tuesday, with some of the royal children there. And, two days later, I was doing a party for Quentin Crewe, miles out in the country, and who should turn up but all the royals again. 'What? Are you here, again?' they said. It was a wonderful feeling. I used to meet them everywhere.

Quentin Crewe's daughter, Candida, who is now grown up, recently wrote an article in one of the glossy magazines about how she'd had a lot of sadness because her parents had split up. But one thing she remembered from her childhood was a birthday party her father and mother had given her with an entertainer. As I had been 'the entertainer' I telephoned Candida and said, 'I read your article and it's Norman Myers, here.' She was so thrilled to talk to me and we had a long chat.

In my files I have a handful of cards that have been clipped together. They all belong to: Kent, The Duchess of, HRH, Kensington Palace, W8, telephone number and Buckinghamshire address. Among the same clutch of cards is: Miss Fiona Pilkington, now Mrs Henderson, lady-in-waiting to the Duchess. I used to do all her parties, as well. She is a charming woman

91

Lieutenant Commander Buckley's name follows – he's the private secretary – and the dates: 1966, December; 1969, April; 1970, April; 1970, 1973, 1974, 1975 and, on other cards, 1979, 1980, 1984. My records show who I met there and how I entertained the children; the puppets for Lady Helen and whether or not the party was held at Ivor Bucks, how many were there and the price of the party. I always noted down every detail.

Through the parties she organised for various charities, the wife of the Honourable James Ogilvy became a good friend of mine. They had a house in Blomfield Road, Little Venice, with half an acre of land behind it, which is very unusual. And so they used to give a lot of charity parties; a lot for the NSPCC. I met Lady Strathallan there quite a lot, and I did her parties, as well.

The card for Mrs Harold Phillips, the daughter Lady Zia Wernher, records the details of the parties for Natasha, now the Duchess of Westminster. They used to live at Luton Hoo, which houses the Wernher collection of porcelain, enamel and other art treasures. As I have said, the Queen used to spend her anniversaries there. The Phillipses were great personal friends of theirs. I was surprised, because when she rang up, she was plain Mrs Phillips and, normally, these people have titles.

The Brands were one of the first parties I did where I met the royal children. They were a very old English family with a lot of history. The children could only have been about four, five and six years old in those days. The Honourable Mrs Brand was connected, in some way, with the Royal Household and I went along to the very first party, early, and offered to help with the table plan and other preparations. She gave me the place names and when I asked where I should put them, I always remember she said, 'Throw them anywhere you like.' And there were six or eight royal children at the party that day.

Justin Beaumont was the nephew of The Clerk to the Course at Royal Ascot Race Course, and I used to meet Prince Andrew at his parties. The royal children who were regulars at parties such as the Brands and Beaumonts were: Prince Andrew, Prince Edward, Viscount Linley and Lady Sarah Armstrong-Jones, the Duchess of

Kent's two children and Princess Alexandra's two children. They were not always there together, but they were quite often at the parties.

The husband of the Honourable Mrs Moffatt – the Honourable Mrs Brand's sister-in-law – was a film producer, as well as being connected to the British aristocracy. He decided to give a party, one day, and to film it for a television documentary about nannies. He asked me to organise it, so we did a party down in Kensington. I had to lay on the food, the novelties, the entertainment, everything. And they invited about 20 or so of the old nannies. This party predates the nanny party I presided over for Nanny Ellis.

It must have been in the sixties, and they had young David Dimbleby and about 30 television people, with scaffolding and other technical props. You've never seen anything like it in your life. Then they filmed the whole party: the children coming in, entertaining them, having their tea, all the nannies there; it must have cost an absolute fortune.

I was told when the programme was going to be transmitted, and that evening I sat expectantly in front of the television. If you'd sneezed, you'd have missed me. That section of the programme must have cost them thousands of pounds, and all they did was show me for two seconds, leading the children into tea. Then they panned round the nannies and went on to show an old nanny of about a hundred, who wasn't at the party, then they flashed over to Paris, to interview this glamorous young nanny. And that, was the Moffat party.

The Honourable Mrs Cayzer was the daughter of one of the Irish nobility and had married into Lord Rotherwick's family. They were big in British and Commonwealth shipping, and they had a beautiful house in Ilchester Place, just by Holland Park. They had three daughters who went to Lady Eden School and I used to do all their parties. In fact, Lady Eden lived opposite the family, at number five, and I used to organise her parties, as well. It was Lady Eden's mother who founded the school, I believe. It's still running and I think Lady Eden is still there.

It's a shame, but a lot of my clients divorce and remarry. I have trouble keeping up with them! I had one titled lady, I can't remember her name, and, for four years running, I organised her children's parties. And, every year, she had a different name. She just married and separated, year after year.

Connected to the Cayzer family is the Honourable Mrs Tollemache. That's an ancient family in the British aristocracy. One of the Cayzer girls, when she grew up, married one of the Tollemaches. They're a country family with big estates and country houses. There's Lord Tollemache and other members of the family.

Lady Kilmarnock was a wonderful woman with whom I was very great friends. She had a house just off Eaton Square, with a big ballroom, and we used to do a lot of parties there. Unfortunately, her husband died, and she was his second wife. The son by his first wife became Lord Kilmarnock, and the ex-Lady Kilmarnock rented the house out for parties, perhaps for extra income. She was a charming, charming lady.

Another party client was Lady Chelsea. The Earl of Cadogan owns the freehold of most of Chelsea, and his son was Lord Chelsea. And, only in the last year or two, the Earl died and Lord Chelsea became Earl of Cadogan. They live in Chelsea Square and I did a lot of parties for them. And, also, in the country, they had a beautiful house near Wantage in Berkshire. A lot of people lived up there: the Hendersons, the lady-in-waiting to the Duchess of Kent, and the Astors lived there.

Unfortunately, Lady Chelsea died and her husband married again, and, I think, the Earl married again, after that. But the children were wonderful. Edward Cadogan was four in 1970, so he must be thirty-four years old. I understand he's about to be married. The first party recorded on the card, is at 30 Pavilion Road in 1968, at Searcy's party town house. Anna was four in 1968 – she must be thirty-six – and Edward was two. Two parties a year; 1968, 1969 ... Ah, they were a lovely crowd, the Chelseas.

7

A Case of Mistaken Identity

Next door to Lord and Lady Chelsea lived the Marquess of Bute, who also had a big estate on the Island of Rothesay. I'd organised a party near there, and we popped across to see the Marquess. We had lunch with him and the family in their home in the island's chief port and holiday resort, Rothesay. The Marquess had built a big hotel, Glenburn, and he put us up there. Sadly, he died recently, and his son, John, the Earl of Dumfries, has succeeded to the Marquisate.

Until recently, I kept in touch with my titled friends by Christmas card. I don't now; I should do, but I don't have the time. I never sent or took birthday cards to the huge number of children I entertained. I knew if I did that once, I'd have to do it all the time, and it would run into hundreds of cards.

I also have the details of a party given on October 21, 1969, by the Honourable Mrs Brand and her sister-in-law, There were 65 children and 40 nannies. We did the food, the novelties, the ice cream cake and more, sherry glasses, as well. The Honourable Mrs Brand's children were Jonathan, five, Rosabel, four and Charlotte, eight.

To handle such an enormous amount of children, I needed the back-up services of either Pat or Vic. And, sometimes, my son Geoffrey would come with me. But he was away at school a lot. Geoffrey loved my parties and, when he was older, he did the photography at these events. And he did quite well, but, unfortunately, he's not interested in carrying on my business. It's gone now. It's finished. It's a shame.

Jennifer, my daughter, was never involved in the party side of the business but assisted me with other aspects of my work. She helped me in the office in the Strand, on the film side of the business. I sent her to one of the top secretarial schools in the country, Lucie Clayton in Knightsbridge – I used to do Lucie Clayton's parties, as well. Jennifer didn't go to boarding school, as her brother had done. She remained in London throughout her childhood. It was a mistake to send Geoffrey to boarding school, with hindsight. But he wanted to go, at the time. It never worked out, but there you are.

Lord Lucan, famous for his disappearance after the murder of his nanny, was a regular client of mine. I organised a lot of parties for Lord and Lady Lucan. I met Lord Lucan many times. He was a very charming person and we sat and talked quite a lot. The last party I did for them was just a week before the murder. The house they lived in, in Lower Belgrave Street, was a very dark little house. They didn't seem to have many lights about, and, in fact, in the hall – and this is what came out later on – there wasn't a light at all. I had to keep going downstairs and opening the door and bringing in people by torch, practically, it was so dark.

Pat was with me at that last party, organising the catering for the afternoon. It's hindsight, but Pat said at the time, because we did all the food, that Sandra, the nanny, and Lady Lucan looked so much alike. They looked like twins, Lady Lucan and Sandra. And when we did the party, we held it upstairs, and I sat with Lord Lucan while the children were having tea.

Unfortunately, a week later, before I was paid, the murder took place. I was interviewed by the police, but I hadn't got much to say. And, eventually, after a great deal of time, I was paid.

I remember the Lucans' three children. I knew young Bingham, the boy, and the two girls very well indeed. Billy Shand Kydd took over the children. Lord Lucan had left a note saying he wanted him to look after the children, which he did. He's another person who's crippled and in a wheelchair. It's very sad. I used to organise the Shand Kydds' parties, as well. They lived in Cambridge Square, just off Marble Arch, and I think his son had leukaemia. Princess Diana's mother left her husband and married a Shand Kydd, I think it was a cousin.

Lady Lucan was very sweet, very quiet and very shy. The children used to like her – I liked her too – and I was very surprised the way things turned out in the end, between her and the children. It's very sad. The boy has been made the Earl of Lucan now. Very recently, they agreed that Lord Lucan was dead, for tax or probate purposes.

Lady Rawlinson was another client I found charming. We got on very well together. But one of my most famous clients was 'Bubbles' Harmsworth. She lived next to Lord Lever, in Eaton Square. She had a flat on the first floor and she had a flat on the lower ground floor, and the first party I ever did for her was in the basement flat garden where they had roundabouts and all sorts of fairground amusements. The party I did was for Jonathan, who's now Viscount Rothermere.

Jonathan was one year old at the time. After that, I organised the family's parties every year; for the three girls, Sarah, Geraldine and Camilla, and Jonathan, for about ten or fifteen years. They're all married now. Geraldine married Lord David Ogilvy, a son of Lord Airlie, the Queen's Lord Chamberlain, and Jonathan, who married recently, now helps to run the family newspaper, the *Daily Mail*.

Viscount Rothermere's father was Vere Harmsworth and the boy became Lord Rothermere when his father died, a few years ago. I used to do the parties for his grandfather, Lord Rothermere, who married an American woman, very late in life. She had six children when he married her and, when he was 70, he produced a son, Esmond Harmsworth. He must be about 20 years old, or more, now. They had the nearest house you can possibly have to Buckingham Palace. If you go up the Mall, towards the Palace and, right at the top, you turn right towards St James's Palace, and go a bit further on, there's an old house there.

When I did the first party there, they didn't even have normal electricity. They had what they call direct current, DC, which is so outdated, it's unbelievable. I had to get special equipment to work with that. Finally, they managed to change the system. It was about the last house in London to be converted to modern electricity.

'Bubbles' Harmsworth, the daughter-in-law of the first Lord Rothermere, was a woman of strong character. I used to do dozens of parties for her at Eaton Square. She was a nice woman, but very difficult. She knew what she wanted and changed her mind 24 times! And we used to do everything for her: the food, the novelties and the entertainment, and we had to see the secretaries and go through lists with her. We'd sit for hours with her, working out the party plans.

She was a real social person. I remember her husband very well too. He was a charming fellow.

Lady Morris of Kenwood is a personal friend of mine. She's the daughter of the late Lord and Lady Janner, and the sister of the present Lord Janner, Greville Janner. Greville and I were friends at the Brady Club; we were both managers at the club after the war. He became chairman of the club the year after I resigned, way back. Ruth Morris is married to Lord Morris of Kenwood, and I used to organise their parties for them.

My index file cards show that the family of Harold, Lord Lever, neighbour of 'Bubbles' Harmsworth in Eaton Square, were clients of mine from 1964 until I retired in 1999. There are six cards, full of details of different parties and with pieces of paper attached, charting each party, not only for the Levers' children, but their grandchildren.

Harold Lever had three magnificent flats, all joined together, at 86 Eaton Square. Mrs Lever, as she was then, had a son, Michael, by her first husband, Mr Zilkha, who owned Mothercare. He was ten when I first did his party in 1964. Recently, I did a party for Michael Zilkha's son Daniel, who's six, when they came over. They live in Houston, Texas, now and we did the party at the Berkeley Hotel.

I organised Michael's parties when he was ten, eleven, twelve and thirteen years of age. In the meantime, in 1966, Lady Lever had three daughters, Isabel, Annabel and Jasmine, and I organised their parties every year. I used to go to their home about three or four times a year. They were wonderful parties, and one of them was the occasion when I had to fly, post-haste, down from Scotland to do the party on a Sunday afternoon.

Lord Lever was a member of Harold Wilson's cabinet and used to entertain other members of the cabinet. He was a brilliant man. He died some time ago, but, last year, I did a party for his grand-daughter.

I am fond of the Lever family and keep in touch with them. I still see them and, in fact, we went to the theatre the other day and Lady Lever was sitting in front of us, and we were very pleased to see each other. When I organised the children's parties at the House of Commons, there was an all-party Ladies' Committee made up of the Conservative, Labour and Liberal parties, and Lady Lever was one of them.

I've seen her every year, for the last few years, with the grand-children at the House of Commons parties. So, we've been in touch for quite a long time. Her daughter Isabel married a doctor and lives in Hampstead and I organised a party for them a short time ago. Jasmine, the youngest, and Annabel live in America now. A wonderful family. One point about the Levers and the Airlies and families like them is that once they had me to do their parties, they didn't want any other entertainer for years and years. It wasn't a question of, 'Oh, I'm fed up with him; I've seen him six times.' Year after year after year, they had me back, and that's the interesting thing about the way I did my work.

Lady Hambledon had a house in Chester Square and another in the country, and she had five boys. They were the W.H. Smith family, and they're very closely connected to the Royal Family. Another person closely connected to the Queen is Lady Susan Hussey, her lady-in-waiting. I used to organise the parties for her children.

One time, I was in Scotland for a golfing holiday with Pat and a couple of friends. We spent a week in Gleneagles and a week in the Boat of Garten, which is a northern Scottish beauty spot with golf courses, and a week at St Andrews. Coming down, one

Sunday morning, from the Boat of Garten to St Andrews, we drove in my car through Balmoral. I had read in the paper that morning that the Queen had just flown up from London to Aberdeen and was staying at Balmoral.

I said to my friends for a joke, 'I know two of the Queen's ladies-in-waiting, Lady Susan Hussey and the Countess of Airlie.' One was a lady-in-waiting and the other was a woman of the bed-chamber, which is even closer to the Queen. I said, 'Let's see if they're there and, maybe, they'll invite us in.'

So, I drove into the courtyard at Balmoral and the police inspector asked what I wanted. I said I happened to be passing and I wondered if Lady Susan or Lady Airlie were in residence because I'd like to say hallo.

The police inspector went away and rang through, and came back a few minutes later. He said, 'I'm awfully sorry, sir, but I spoke to Lady Susan and she said she's delighted to hear from you and she apologises, but would you mind if she didn't come out because they've just arrived and they're unpacking.' And there was I, imagining her and the Queen opening up the luggage and hanging things up!

But names can open doors, and gates, on occasions. Pat and I used to enjoy a holiday in Spain, every year with friends. One year we were there, and the BBC had started *El Dorado*, a new soap opera, and built a whole village in the mountains. Everybody was going mad about it and we were in the region. The village was very difficult to find and we circled miles. It was tucked away but we finally found it, after miles of driving around. We drove up to the studio gate, where a commissionaire greeted us. I asked if it were possible to come in and look around, and he said he was sorry but it wasn't possible without special permission because they were shooting scenes.

One of our friends, in particular, was very disappointed. She watched the programme regularly on television and had looked forward to seeing the set. I said to her, 'Let me try something.' I went back to the gate and said, 'I'm a friend of the chairman of the BBC, Marmaduke Hussey.' He was Lady Susan's husband. The commissionaire asked me to wait while he rang through. He came back and said, 'Would you like to come in, sir?' and we got the

VIP treatment. The producer came and showed us all around. We had lunch there and had a fabulous time. And that was thanks to Lady Susan.

The first lady-in-waiting to the Queen to use my party services was Lady Margaret Hay. I didn't realise her importance at the time, otherwise I would have done more to project myself.

Lady Peel was another client I found charming when she asked me to organise her son's party in Richmond in Yorkshire, and Pat and I were guests at the house overnight, since the journey was over 400 miles, there and back.

Lord and Lady Pembroke lived at Wilton House, the enormous estate in Salisbury, Wiltshire. I think I did two parties for them, one in Salisbury and one in London. Unfortunately, the couple divorced and the parties stopped.

I often organised parties for the children of a first marriage, then for those of the parents' subsequent marriages; then, again, for those children's children, and the children of their second marriages.

The network is enormous. People say I'm like a *Debrett's*; I can remember who married who. I can connect any name on my thousands of index cards with other family names on other cards. To me, all these people are personalities, and I have had great pleasure in meeting them all – because they accepted me as an equal and we got on very well.

Lady Tryon was, for me, a memorable character. Lord and Lady Tryon were great friends of Prince Charles, and great friends of a lot of my clients, and I believe the Duchess of Gloucester was a particular friend of Lady Tryon. She had an unusual name: Kanga, because she was Australian, and they had one son, whose parties I used to organise.

There is an index card for the Honourable Mrs Nicholas Robertson, whose boy, Struan, went to boarding school at Heathfield with Prince Edward. I used to take his birthday cake to him, all the way down from London to the school. There were battleship birthday cakes, horse birthday cakes, Concorde cakes and a football pitch cake. Every year, I'd get the most marvellous cakes for him and I still see friends of the family at Royal Ascot, every year. The Honourable Mrs Robertson was so dependent on me that I used to provide, with expertise, Christmas lunches and dinner parties. If she gave a dinner party, she couldn't organise it herself, so I'd get the necessary things sent over. For instance, one card reads: 'February 9, 1973, home lunch, dinner via Antoinette's, £60'.

The Honourable Mrs Robertson moved from Pont Street to South Eaton Place, next door to a great friend of the Queen. The Queen used to have lunch in the garden there. The Queen visits a lot of people privately. But I never heard gossip or anecdotes about the Royal Family from their friends, and I never mentioned anything myself. Everyone surrounding royalty has always been most discreet. It's why I was always chosen for the birthday parties. I never used to talk about anyone.

Tiggy Legge Bourke, who organised many parties in London and often asked me to take care of the entertainments, was part of the royal scene. She gave me several parties. The last time I saw Diana, Princess of Wales was when I organised a children's party for Lord King, the chairman of British Airways. Tiggy asked me to do the party at 75 Eaton Square, and Princess Diana, who was a great friend of Lord King's daughter, was there with Prince William and Prince Harry.

I remember the Princess as a very beautiful woman. She loved children and she loved to sit and watch the parties, particularly Vic's Punch and Judy shows. She used to sit on the floor, in front of me. I think I did the egg trick with her, and asked her to throw the egg in the air. I have a thank-you letter from Lady King, dated December, 1986, thanking me for my help and the trouble I took with their party. I almost always received a letter of thanks for my services, either from the child or the parent, showing their appreciation for all I done.

Princess Diana had been a teacher at Young England, the nursery school in Pimlico. When she married, she became god-mother to the child of a client of mine. The first time I saw her, she was expecting Prince William. I was told the Princess of Wales was coming to the party and I was introduced to her. She was just like all the other mothers, walking around and serving tea. Just a natural, normal, lovely person. I saw Princess Diana about half a dozen times, mostly when her children were between three and eight years old. After that, the boys were away at boarding school.

It was the same with Princes Andrew and Edward: I saw them, mostly, when they were aged between five and eight, before they went off to boarding school. Most of their friends went off to school and they had their parties at the Palace. I was never invited to organise the parties at the Palace, which I would have loved to have done. I understand the children had a film or a magician, but little else, and I regret not having had the opportunity to entertain the princes in their own home.

When I went to the country to give a party for Lord and Lady Porchester, the Earl of Carnarvon's son and daughter-in-law, I met Prince Andrew there with Miss Peebles, the governess. I used to see Miss Peebles and Prince Andrew together at parties quite often. She would be there with him if Mabel couldn't come. Mabel was mostly looking after Prince Edward, I think. Miss Peebles was a charming Scottish woman and we became very friendly. Geoffrey, my son, used to come to the parties, as well, and he and Prince Andrew got on quite well; they were about six and seven years old at that time. Miss Peebles was going to invite us to tea at the Palace but, unfortunately, she died, very young. It's the only time I've sent a wreath to a funeral, and that was to Windsor Castle.

Not only the names, but also the addresses of my clients for over nearly 50 years are imprinted on my mind. Mention Mrs Faber, and I will tell you she lived at 3 Chester Square, opposite the current home of Baroness Thatcher. When I used to go to the Fabers, they were so pleased to see me and made me very much at home. I used to do the parties and then sit down with them and talk.

I also sat and talked with Harold Macmillan, Mrs Faber's father, at many of the family parties. I used to have a lot of discussions with Macmillan on politics; on subjects like Harold Wilson, which is understandable, because Harold Wilson was the Labour leader and Macmillan was, of course, the former Conservative prime minister.

My clients came from a variety of international backgrounds. Lady Dufferin and Ava came from an Irish family background, but the wife of Lord Duncan Sandys, the politician, was French. She's a marvellous person, and we got on very well together. They had a lovely house in Vincent Square, opposite Westminster School, and what I liked about it was, in the loo, they had all the original cartoons the newspapers had published about him.

A few years ago, Lady Sainsbury, Sir Tim Sainsbury's wife, bought Lord Sandys' house and I organised a party there for her granddaughter. We go back to the same house, time and again. Not only do I give parties for clients who may divorce and remarry and have another family, and for their children, but I often return to the house of a former client when it has been sold to another client. I know every turning, every road, every house in SW1, SW3 and the other wealthy boroughs.

Lord and Lady Bathurst had an enormous estate in the West Country where I organised a number of parties. But it was while we were attending a garden party at Lady Beaumont's very large house in Hampstead that Pat and I received our own honorary titles.

Lord Beaumont was the president of the Liberal Party and Pat and I met and talked to a number of interesting people at his garden party, that day. One guest asked who we were and I volunteered our names, Norman and Pat Myers. After that, he kept calling us Lord and Lady Myers! And we didn't have the heart to correct our fellow-guest.

I organised parties for Lord Bath when he was a child. The old Lord Bath asked us down to Longleat, his estate in Wiltshire, and wanted a particular Laurel and Hardy feature film, which we brought and showed. This is going back a long time. We did practically all the big estates, Longleat, Wilton, Woburn, Hatfield House . . .

Another country house I visited regularly was the home of Countess Beatty and her daughter, Miranda. On average, the number of children in these titled families was two or three, which kept me busy enough. There were exceptions. The Airlies had six children, the Dudleys had six and a lot of people had four; generally speaking, it was between two and four.

Other well-known names in my card system are: Lady Bristol at Ickworth House in Suffolk, Lady Rotherwick of the Cayzer family in Scotland and, later, the estate next to Blenheim Palace, where Winston Churchill is buried. Randolph, Sir Winston Churchill's son, was the only one of the Churchill family for whom I organised a party. I used to meet Churchill's grandson, Winston, and, later, his child, Randolph, at a lot of parties, but I never did their parties.

Several of my clients have suffered because of male succession to the family title. For instance, Lady Anne Tennant, now Lady Glenconner, was one of four daughters of the Earl of Leicester. When her father died, the family had to move out of their stately home and cousins took over the estate, because there was no male heir. The same thing happened with the Duke of Norfolk, the premier duke of England. When he died, his daughters had to move out and their cousins took their place.

One of the Duke of Norfolk's daughters married David Frost, the TV producer. I once organised the entertainment for one of David Frost's large parties in Egerton Terrace, Knightsbridge, before he married. It was a large three-storey house. I engaged a caricaturist for the first floor, a palmist to read hands on the second floor and a friend of mine, a member of the Magic Circle called Jack Mayes, doing close-table magic on the top storey. I remember the Two Ronnies being very impressed with the magician. Many of my clients were guests at the party and several of them came over and asked me, quietly, if they could see the palmist without queuing. The woman was such a success, there was a queue to see her, all night.

As well as aristocracy and business tycoons, I have also entertained international diplomats, and their children. The Iranian ambassador at one time was the son-in-law of the Shah of Persia. The ambassador's children attended Lady Eden School, where so many diplomats' offspring went, and he was so busy with the turbulent affairs of his country that he had no time to give parties for his children. He used to hold two parties a year for his daughter, which I did, at the embassy. We used to bring in everything, all the food, and do the lot. The Iranian Embassy was soon to be famous for its hostage siege, in which the SAS stormed the building and rescued the hostages. I used to go to the embassy quite a lot, so I know it inside out.

I was also a regular at the Belgian Embassy. I did the Christmas parties there for about ten years. It's at the corner of Belgrave Square. The German Embassy's on one corner and the Belgian Embassy is on the other. Security wasn't a big issue for visitors in the sixties and the early seventies; it was not until the end of the century that it was tightened, in the wake of major incidents around the world. I may have been 'checked out', but I have never knowingly been subject to a security check.

I also gave a children's party at the Israeli Embassy. But nothing happened, as far as I know. It's the first house in Kensington Palace Gardens, where all the embassies are. The Israeli Embassy is, as you come in from Kensington, and the last house on the right, in Bayswater, is the Russian Embassy. But I never crossed the threshold of the then Soviet building and I wonder if they ever had parties.

The Israeli ambassador lived in Avenue Road, Regent's Park, but the party at the embassy was not especially for his children; it was probably for the children of the staff. The Senegalese ambassador also rang me to ask me to arrange a party. I also did one for the Argentinian Embassy and the Venezuelan Embassy. With the Jordanian ambassador, Alkaylani, I used to do the parties privately, in Ennismore Gardens. His son, Jaffah, was eight years old when I first went there, and his other child was six and I organised parties several years running. The ambassador was a very nice chap, very friendly.

Another regular client for parties was the Nigerian ambassador in his residence in 'Millionaires' Row' in Kensington Gardens. As at the Iranian Embassy, we were asked to do everything, including food and novelties. I entertained many of the ambassador's compatriots there, until, one day, there was a coup and everyone disappeared from the scene. A few years ago, at Christmas, I was asked to do two parties for Chief Abiola, the newly-elected

Nigerian president, whose children I had entertained in London the previous year. But a few days before the first of the parties, his wife telephoned me and cancelled the two dates. Her husband had returned to Nigeria, she told me, to take up his new post as head of government, and was immediately arrested upon his arrival. In the early summer of 1996, Mr Abiola was found dead in Lagos, the capital of Nigeria. They were a lovely family, with a big house in Hendon, in north London.

I often did charity children's parties at a reduced rate or for free, or gave a donation. I used to take Vic with me. One such event, in 1999, was the Bosnia Lifeline for HRH Crown Princess Catherine of Yugoslavia, for which I received a heartfelt thank-you letter on the most exquisite notepaper.

One of the most interesting places in London, for me, is the Chelsea Physic Garden at the beginning of Cheyne Walk. It was founded in 1673 by the Royal Society of Apothecaries, and is the oldest botanical garden in the country after the garden at Oxford. I've been there many times, and I did a party there for the Heart Foundation. They gave a party for children who'd been very brave in their illness. The children had submitted paintings for a Christmas calendar and the Foundation chose the 12 best pictures to go in the calendar. The children who'd done the paintings, and their parents, were invited to the Physic Garden and I entertained them.

The Save the Children Fund was another charity I was involved in. People who work for the various charities sell party tickets to other people, in order to raise money for their cause. They have a Christmas party or an Easter party, and the tickets cost X amount and the money goes to the Kosovo Fund or the Save the Children Fund or whichever fund has organised the party.

This is how they raise money: they have suppers, dinners and balls, and the children's parties are another way of doing this. They hold these at venues such as the Dorchester, Claridges and the Savoy; one of them, Princess Diana's Birthright charity, used to be held at the General Medical centre in Regent's Park. All the different illnesses, such as cystic fibrosis, multiple sclerosis and

107

cancer, have charities and their committees raise money through various events, including children's parties.

I've done several large parties for the Multiple Dystrophy Group of the Royal Courts of Justice, at The Old Hall, Lincoln's Inn, and The Hall at the Temple, both in summer and winter. I also support their cheese and wine functions at the Great Hall in Lincoln's Inn, every year; they had a wonderful committee.

The Invalid Children's Aid Association children's party was held at the Savoy, every year in January. There could be 200 or 300 children at these parties. The Belgrave Fair for the NSPCC was held annually, in the summer, in the middle of Belgrave Square. There were all sorts of stalls from many different organisations and, occasionally, they would ask us to put on a Punch and Judy show in one corner.

Although Vic worked independently, the majority of his bookings came through my parties. If I had two parties that day, Vic used to do the other party. He would do the games, magic, Punch and Judy and ventriloquist puppets. He had Hamilton, his naughty boy puppet, and he'd do a quarter of an hour warm-up with the puppet before he did the Punch and Judy show. It was very good. Vic is a very good entertainer.

One of my big charity parties each year was at the House of Commons for the Westminster Medical School Research Trust. I'd been doing that for about 30 years, but a new policy was introduced by the Banqueting Department of the House of Commons in 1997, when Labour became the new Government, which meant that any party held in the Commons had to be connected to the House. If the party wasn't connected, the large discount for the tea, which had been given to the Charitable Trust in recent years, was cancelled. This new policy, plus the low selling price of the tickets, made the Easter parties uneconomical. The profit was so small that it wasn't worth the effort we'd all put in every year to make the event such a success.

The parties were organised by the Palace of Westminster All-Party Ladies' Committee, with Viscountess Whitelaw, Lady Barber and Lady Irving of Lairg, Lady Trafford and Lady Wigoder. It was the best party of the year, for both children and adults, and I used to tell the chaps at the golf club, quite rightly,

108

that it was the finest party in London. The tickets were relatively cheap and the children used to come along to the House of Commons Members' and Strangers' Dining Room and have games before tea. They used to have an excellent tea, followed by the entertainment, either Punch and Judy or films or magic, and we had people like Paul Daniels doing a turn.

The parties took place at Easter; before that, it had been Christmas, but too many people were away at that time. We sold tickets several weeks in advance and we usually had between 180 and 240 adults and children attending. I kept meticulous notes of the different types of entertainment and we sometimes had an Easter egg or Easter bonnet competition. The older children took part in a Parliamentary quiz and there were excellent prizes.

The last three parties had a London theme. The committee invited the Pearly King and Queen of Southwark, a yeoman warder from the Tower of London, a guardsman from the Palace Guard in a bearskin hat, and a Chelsea Pensioner. These colourfully attired people delighted the children, especially when they joined in the games in full costume.

In the early days, when the Fund had a strong committee, a lot of television stars came along and we used to tell the children to bring their autograph books. On top of that, while we were entertaining the children, friends of the MPs and peers in the House of Lords used to take people on tours of the Commons and the Lords. So, it was wonderful for the grown-ups as well, and, at the end, the children got a present and a balloon to go home with.

I started doing the Westminster Hospital Research Fund parties about 30 years ago at Westminster Hospital at the back of Victoria Street. Then they had the All-Party Ladies' Committee, and, year after year, we did the parties at the House of Commons. In 1999 the committee, with great respect, wasn't a powerful committee and couldn't raise enough money, and it was the first year we didn't do it. They should have had a brochure or a big raffle, instead of a small one, in the House itself, that afternoon. It's a shame but there we are.

Once, I organised a children's party for adults. It was for an

Italian count in Knightsbridge. All the parents arrived dressed as children, the mothers in little skirts and tops and the men in short trousers. We put on Laurel and Hardy cartoons, and then we went home!

Very different clients were the Count and Countess Bernadotte of Wisborg. I have a pack of index cards for this regular customer, from 1986, when the boys, Edward and Oscar, were three and four respectively, and the daughter, Astrid, was also quite young. The Count was the cousin of the King of Sweden and his father was a United Nations ambassador, who was unfortunately assassinated. We got on very well with him and his wife and we did a lot of parties for them. They lived opposite the Buccleuchs' house in Kensington and I used to do their parties around Christmas time. What was so lovely was that, placed on top of the piano, were the Christmas cards of practically all the crowned heads of Europe. And yet, they were such a nice couple, so normal, and always greeted me and asked me inside in such a friendly way. They never had anyone but me to entertain the children, that's what I liked about it.

I liked to provide entertainment for my clients' parties every year; it was a true sign of customer satisfaction, and the majority of my clients were 'repeats'. When I began my career, showing films in village halls around the country, I once showed some films in a village called Chiddingfold, in Surrey. A few years ago I met somebody who has the amazing name of Mrs Bagewell-Purefoy, and she was the daughter of a client called Gilroy, for whom I used to organise parties in Chiddingfold, way back.

Renewed connections such as this have brought added satisfaction over the years. Mrs Jeremy Bagewell-Purefoy, formerly Gilroy, moved to London, where I organised parties for her children, Oliver and Natasha.

Like many well-to-do families, the Bagewell-Purefoys moved across the river, to the Clapham area in SW4. Times were changing and so were party locations, and so was my clientele. A new breed of aristocracy was asking for my services, and I was as delighted to meet these glamorous people as I was my old friends, the dowager duchesses.

8

The New Aristocracy

Another famous client of mine was the interior designer Nina Campbell. I did masses of parties for her, I began organising her children's parties in 1984, when she lived in Drayton Gardens, SW7, and, later, when she married again and moved to Chelsea Park Gardens. In my files are details of the films I showed and the different cakes I organised for her children.

Squirrel War was a film I used to show, a half-hour colour cartoon, ideal for children. Parents never needed to discuss the films in advance, they trusted me completely Occasionally, they'd say they wanted a cowboy film or a Laurel and Hardy film, but they knew I kept a list of what I'd shown at different parties, and they knew I wouldn't repeat myself, unless the client particularly asked for something.

Henrietta and Max Koenig, the children of Nina Koenig, formerly Campbell, are now young adults and often featured in the social columns. The family moved to various addresses in SW1 and SW3 over the years, which were my main working areas. When I began my career in entertainment, I lived in north London and I didn't know west London very well, at all. At some stage, I thought of moving there, so I wouldn't have to keep travelling back and forth, but it wasn't worth it. My roots and family are north of the park.

The name Nikkah is not immediately recognisable to most people, but the international jewellers Van Kleef and Arpel are owned by the Nikkah family of SW7. They had an enormous estate in Oxfordshire. I used to hire a coach and take the children up there for the parties.

111

Another name not well known was Kapoor. She was an Indian princess, and they lived in a fabulous house in Charles Street, Mayfair. They were wonderful people and we got on well together.

I organised Alexandra, 'Tiggy' Legge Bourke's own parties, when she was a child. I see from my files that, in 1972 she had the game of 'Pirates', three boxes of crackers and the ever-popular *Squirrel War* film, and Vic was there with his Punch and Judy show. Tiggy's sister, Zara, and her brother, Harry – now a courtier or aide-de-camp to one of the royals – were also at the parties, which took place on the family's estate in Wales, to which I used to travel.

In my folder of thank-you letters is one from Tiggy's mother Sian Legge Bourke, dated March 24, 1976, thanking me for organising Harry's party. She writes that it was a great success and Harry and everyone, including the nannies, enjoyed every moment of it. She also thanks my son Geoffrey for his help and looks forward to me organising the next parties for her daughters.

There is a story behind every client, but not always one that can be told. I organised a lot of parties for the Schilds. The daughter, Annabel, was kidnapped by Corsican bandits when she was grown up. I knew her very well.

Baroness Thyssen was another memorable client. Her husband had one of the greatest art collections in the world. I organised parties for him in Chester Square, and one at the estate in Oxfordshire. Their son, Alexander, went to the famous Dragon prep school and the Baroness had the whole of the boy's form to the party. At the end of the party, Baroness Thyssen showed me over their house. It was like a museum, with all these fantastic paintings. And they were very nice people.

The estate was bought by Sir Anthony Bamford, the owner of the public company, JCB. The first year I did his party, I had to go way out into the country. The following year, his secretary rang me and offered to have me collected by helicopter to be taken to the party. Unfortunately, I was engaged that particular day, so no helicopter ride!

112

Another pupil of the Dragon school was the son of the TV presenter and author of *The Naked Ape*, Desmond Morris. I organised his parties in Banbury Road, Oxford, for years and years and his wife and Pat and I got very friendly, and he signed his book for me, with my name. His house was full of books and, I remember, it was a very unusual home. It was an old house with lots of wonderful rooms and an enormous indoor swimming pool, and he used to have swimming parties.

Dr Morris and I used to sit down for a drink and a talk after the parties and I found him an interesting and friendly person. What was also interesting was that a lot of the parents who came at the end of the party were professors and dons from the colleges at Oxford University, and it was wonderful to talk to these people.

I also have an index card for Princess Ernst August Hanover, the first wife of the husband of Princess Caroline of Monaco. They lived in Tregunter Road, SW10. Their son, Christian, was five years old in 1990 when I organised his party and their other son, Ernst, was the first born. I met their father, the Prince, many times and found him charming.

Lady Camilla Dempster, the wife of the columnist Nigel Dempster, was another of my clients. She is the daughter of the Duke of Leeds. I used to do her children's parties before she married him – he's her second husband. And I continued to do the parties when they married and lived at Cadogan Gardens.

My client cards have dates stretching back as far as 1958: a Mrs Pearson in Hyde Park Gate, SW7, has the original 'KNI' for Knightsbridge as part of her phone number. There are entries for her, from that date, for nearly every year of the sixties, one entry in the seventies and another in 1991. I used to work in guineas, and the cards have the old, pre-decimal prices on them.

The Marquess of Tavistock's brother, Lord Russell, was another regular client of mine, and I organised parties with Lady Frances Russell for their daughter, Czarina, who was eight years old in 1983. She was a beautiful girl and we did lots of parties in the seventies and eighties for them in SW7. That was until, one day, I received a letter from Lady Russell, regretting her daughter had become too old for such parties and adding that the family would miss me.

By the 1970s the pop star was part of the establishment. The Beatles and the Rolling Stones headed the new aristocracy, and they booked my party services.

I used to organise children's parties for Mick and Bianca Jagger at San Lorenzo, at 22 Beauchamp Place, Knightsbridge, in the afternoons, downstairs, when the restaurant was empty. I think Jade Jagger was three, four, five and six years old, and Bianca Jagger was there, sitting with the children. Jade was a very nice child and, as far as I remember, most of the children who came to her parties were from her school. Jade was six in 1977, and Vic came with me to do the Punch and Judy show. I have very full notes on the parties and each date is around October the 19th and 21st. One year, I've noted 'In America for birthday'. The address for Mr and Mrs Jagger is Cheyne Walk, Chelsea, and he's still there. It's his office.

As I mentioned before, Mick Jagger's financial adviser was Prince Loewenstein. He lived in Holland Park and had two sons and a daughter, Princess Theodora, and I organised their parties for several years. Recently, Theodora married and I sent her a letter of congratulations. She sent me a delightful letter, thanking me and telling me how much she'd enjoyed her birthday parties when she was young.

Next door to Mick Jagger, in Cheyne Walk, lived Paul Getty Jnr. I organised a party for the Gettys' children, and the wife and all the guests were sitting on enormous soft cushions.

At the height of the Beatles' fame, I was asked to organise parties for the group's drummer, Ringo Starr. They were for his son Zak, at their home in Highgate, and the first time I went there, I was amazed at the reaction of the parents who came to collect their offspring at the end of the party. It was as if they'd come into the presence of the Pope. They were overawed, just to be in the house. Of course, as I was used to a range of clients, so pop stars, for me were simply 'business as usual'.

Another time, Ringo asked me to organise a party at John Lennon's home in Ascot. I think it was called Tittinghurst, an enormous estate. John Lennon wasn't there; I think he was in

America, by then, and he'd lent his home to Ringo. We had the party in the garden, I remember, it was such nice weather.

When the party had ended, Paul McCartney appeared and sat and chatted with Ringo, me, my son Geoffrey and Geoffrey's friend. Geoffrey must have been about seven or eight years old, and he and his friend were big fans of the 'Fab Four'. Obviously, I could not be mistaken for a pop star, and Paul McCartney asked me if I was an accountant or a solicitor. The two Beatles sat in the kitchen for hours, singing and playing their instruments, and Geoffrey and I thoroughly enjoyed ourselves. It was a wonderful evening.

Another star from Liverpool was Cilla Black, later to become a TV personality. She asked me to organise several parties for her at her home in Denham, Buckinghamshire. She still lives there. It's a beautiful house.

Keith Moon, the eccentric and tragic drummer of The Who pop group, was another regular client. I made contact with him through Ringo Starr. He lived in an ultra-modern designer home in Chertsey, Surrey, called Tara House. You went into the sitting room, and you had to walk down into a pit, and that's where you sat. A most unusual place. The bizarre thing was, all the time I was doing parties for the daughter, Mandy, and her cousin, Dermott, her father was tearing around the garden, smashing up his Maserati cars. I did Dermott and Mandy's parties almost every year, until 1976. The last parties were organised in East Sheen, where the drummer's estranged wife lived. Keith Moon died of a drug overdose in 1978, aged 32.

The actor Bill Oddie, of *The Goodies* fame, was a client I remember with especial pleasure. A charming person. They lived in south Hampstead and had a lovely daughter, who is now the actress Kate Hardie. Kate's parents divorced but I remember them as being a very friendly couple.

The acting profession also used my services regularly, and another household name who became a client was the actor Sir John Mills. We organised a party for his daughter Hayley, the child star, when she was about six or seven; probably in their house in Richmond.

I also organised parties for the actress Anna Massey, daughter of the American film star Raymond Massey. Her married name was Mrs Huggins, although she divorced, and her child's name was David. We held the party at Searcy's 30 Pavilion Road house, and we had 50 children.

As the Swinging Sixties began in London, I entertained more and more children of the international jet set. I did various parties for the Kennedy clan. Princess Lee Radziwill, Jackie Kennedy's sister, telephoned me after her son had seen me at a party. She was married to Prince Stas Radziwill and they lived in Buckingham Gate, at the side of Buckingham Palace, and she asked me to do their son's party. This led to me organising another party for President Kennedy's press secretary, and as a result I did several other parties for the American hierarchy when they came to London.

When Lauren Bacall came to London to star in *The Pyjama Game*, she asked me to do the birthday party for her ten-year-old son by Jason Robards. The interesting thing is, in *The Pyjama Game* or whenever you see her, she's the most beautiful blonde, beautifully dressed, made-up and elegant person. When she asked me to come and see her at her rented house in Kensington, she came down in her dressing gown and with no make-up on. But she had presence; she was a tall woman with a husky voice. We had a wonderful conversation, just talking generally, and I found she was a very relaxed and natural person. Vic came with me and we did a Punch and Judy show.

Peter Sellers had a party at Searcy's in Pavilion Road for his daughter, one Christmas, when he was married to Lord Mancroft's daughter, Miranda. He bought the whole of one of the windows of Harrods, with the reindeers in it and everything, and took it all down to the party. He was always mad on photography, and he was dancing around that place the whole day with about six cameras round his neck.

Sometimes things didn't go according to plan and I had to improvise. On one particular occasion, the clients had two daughters and the party was on a Sunday afternoon. Unfortunately, it was one of

Christopher
Heseltine and
Concorde cake

Lady Sieff and me

Summer party at Lady Benton-Jones' in Lincolnshire

HAPPY: Harry and William have fun

The Royal Court Jeste

HE'S THE MAN WHO MAKES WILLS AND HARRY LAUGH

PRINCESS DIANA sat laughing in delight the day her cheeky son Prince William came down to earth with a bump.

And William and his little brother Prince Harry were having a wonderful time too.

It happened at a children's birthday party at the home of one of Diana's old school friends. The Princess was in such relaxed mood that she didn't have her royal detective around. She helped make the tea, then sat cross-legged on the floor with about twenty other mums to enjoy the fun.

William quickly got into the spirit of things. Watched by his admiring mother, he sat down on the floor so smartly that he won first prize in a game of musical bumps.

The man who put the royal visitors so much at ease at the birthday bash last Christmas was a quietly-spoken character in a sober grey suit.

And he knows exactly how to do it, for behind the shy exterior of Norman Myers is a sense of impish fun which has delighted two generations of royal children.

Norman is the top people's entertainer whose skills have bewitched four princes — Andrew, Edward, William and Harry — and a host of society people's tots.

by BRYAN ROSTRON

UNCLE Norman, as they all call him, is a magical master of ceremonies. He comes along with his "assistant" Monty the Monkey and introduces them to Punch and Judy and a world of wonderful tricks and fun.

He seems to adore Princess Diana's mischievous youngsters just as much as they love him.

He says: "They are lovely, charming children. Very ordinary, not at all stand-offish.

"William is not arrogant as some people have said.

"He's lively, yes, but a sweet, natural little lad and he fits in marvellously with other children.

"William's like Andrew, extrovert and a bit cheeky. But a happy person and utterly delightful.

"Harry's more like Edward, more shy and introverted.

"They don't get singled out for special treatment. They love all the same sort of things as the other kids.

"At that birthday party William and Harry enjoyed

everything and really got involved."

They played Pass the Parcel, Musical Statues and Simon Says and sang songs such as The Farmer's in his Den.

They were in their element. So was Norman, who has been making children laugh since he gave up studying law 35 years ago.

These days he boasts a list of tiny-tot clients that reads like a toytown Debrett's.

He has entertained a dazzling star cast of show-biz types, among them Ringo Starr, Lauren Bacall and Sir John Mills.

Well, their children, really — though the parents are usually hovering in the background.

HE also entranced the children of Princess Margaret's great friend Lord Glenconner. And that was when he met Nanny Barnes, who became nanny to William and Harry.

The nannies, that strange "mafia" from the world of Upstairs, Downstairs, were his greatest allies.

If they liked Norman, the word got round the very best households.

He recalls: "When I started out I met Nanny

Lightbody, who'd been nanny to the Queen."

His first royal invitation was in 1966. The Duke and Duchess of Kent summoned him to bring his bag of tricks and Monty the Monkey to Iver in Buckinghamshire for a party in honour of their son, the Earl of St Andrews.

Then in 1969, he was invited back to perform for Lady Helen Windsor's fifth birthday — and again for her sixth birthday.

The two young princes, Andrew and Edward, were there.

"Andrew was a delightful extrovert," says Norman affectionately.

Though he is now the

Duke of York, Andrew h never forgotten those ki dies' parties with Mon the Monkey.

When Norman wrote congratulate him on h marriage, the Duke repli that he remembered the with great pleasure.

"Andrew could cheeky," admits Norma whose North London hom is currently festooned wi cards for his recent silv wedding anniversary.

"Take the game Th Farmer's in his De Everyone has to pic someone out to act som thing out.

"Someone chose A

6 William is like Prince Andrew, extrovert and a bit cheeky 9

NTMENT:
E PARTIES

CHEEKY: Andrew

SHY: Prince Edward

ACTING UP: Lord Linley

PARTYING: Lady Helen

MONKEY BUSINESS: Entertainer Norman Myers.   Picture: PETER STONE

as a dog — so he me as a bone!
ndrew was very rd, Edward more shy etiring.
did all their friends' rs. Sometimes I l see the princes two ree times a week. I have entertained 60 to 30 times.
at they've become so more informal since days.
drew used to come rties with his gover- Miss P., and Edward to come with his y, Mabel.
e Queen and Prince never came. It sim-

ply wasn't done. Now it's so different.
Norman may deserve some of the credit for giving Prince Edward his yen for the stage.
One of his games, called I Want To Be An Actor, was specially designed to "bring out" shy young-sters.

TIMID children would be given some dramatic lines to act out a little scene, sometimes with a girl.
"But I can't say that I spotted Prince Edward's

acting talent at that age, I must admit," laughs Nor-man.
"On the other hand I thought David Linley was rather good as an actor as a child.
"He was another very shy boy and I remember he enjoyed acting."
Norman recently met David, Princess Mar-garet's eldest son, again at a party.
But this time it was one strictly for adults — thrown by the Queen's cousin Lady Elizabeth Anson.
These days Linley runs a thriving furniture busi-

ness, but Norman remem-bers him better as the shy young lad who had to be coaxed out of a corner.
And he remembers the Duke of York as a cheeky five-year-old rather than a dashing serviceman.

LIKE all those who stay in royal favour year after year, Norman Myers does not court public-ity.
He offers his services via a tiny ad in the upper-crust magazine Harpers & Queen.
It simply says: "The finest name in children's entertainment — Games, Films, Magic, Punch and Judy, Puppets."
Norman likes the old-fashioned approach. He has two grandchildren Daniel and Mark, and reckons kids still prefer the traditional games.
Reluctantly, in recent years he has had to intro-duce discos for the over-eights. But he still relies on games, magic and car-toon films which he orga-nises himself.
For thirty years he's been helped by "Uncle" Vic Weldon, who does the Punch and Judy and a ventriloquist turn with a boy dummy called Hamil-ton.
Norman says: "I am

really quite shy with adults, but I love chil-dren.
"I am a child at heart and I deal with them as equals.
"I don't dress up, put on a red nose and shout: 'Ha! Ha! Ha! Hello little chil-dren!'
"I don't use a lot of props. I just aim to get the children happy and cheer-ful.
"The parents like me too because I don't get the children too excited."

HIS magic tricks are very simple. "A disappearing egg, for example, and my magic words, 'Chitty-chitty-bang-bang'. That's all you need.
"The atmosphere's the thing. Fun and games!"
Everyone gets the same show. For £85, plus op-tional extras, you are guaranteed to be passing the parcel with some very socially elevated tots.
"There's a secret to get-ting on with kids," re-flected Norman as he prepared to set off for a lunchtime birthday party.
"You have to treat them as normal, Royal or not."

Sir James and Lady
Annabel Goldsmith
with Zak and friends

King Constantine of
Greece and me

Pat and I

the hottest of summer days and many of the invited children's parents rang to say they were unable to come, as the family were going out for the day. I arrived for the appointment, early as usual. I never liked my clients to worry about me not turning up, so I always arrived between 30 and 60 minutes early.

We waited for the rest of the invited children to turn up. We waited and waited. Not one other child appeared; it was just the two party girls and me. So, I carried on with the entertainments, as usual, and the girls thoroughly enjoyed themselves. Unfortunately, the mother had forgotten to order a birthday cake. I hunted about the kitchen and looked in the larder and found a small piece of cake, left over from the previous day. I wrapped it in coloured paper and put my magic candles on it and we all sang the 'Happy Birthday' sing-song lustily.

Then there was the time I organised a party for Harold Macmillan's grandchildren, Mrs Faber's boys. Unfortunately, on the previous day, they'd been stricken with a children's illness, such as measles or chicken pox, and the party was cancelled. I was a regular party-giver at the Fabers and the parents knew their children would be disappointed at missing the entertainment, so they invited me to their home, all the same, and I entertained the two boys, in my usual fashion.

A famous property dealer of that era was 'Black Jack' Dellal. Mr and Mrs Dellal lived in Lowndes Square, Belgravia, and had five children. I organised parties for them when they were young, and then for the Dellals' grandchildren in the late seventies. On one occasion, I was entertaining some of the grandchildren and their friends in Wimbledon, and all was going well. The children had been invited to come in fancy dress and all had done so, except one small boy of five. When I asked the boy why he wasn't dressed up like the others, he replied, 'I don't have to; my father is Superman.'

I laughed at this and said, 'In that case, he must be a big, strong daddy.' Later that day, just before tea, the boy's father walked into the room. It was indeed Superman: the actor, Christopher Reeve, who was in England to promote his latest Superman film. My face went quite red, but Christopher Reeve sat down with his boy, cross-legged on the floor, in front of me, and watched my magic act.

＊　＊　＊

I have entertained children all over London and the British Isles.
Wherever you go, there are wonderful houses with objets d'art
inside. And there are certain houses in London with quite a bit of
land attached, and you don't realise it. Lady Annabel Goldsmith's
first house in Kensington had half an acre of land, Evelyn de
Rothschild's home in Holland Park had the same amount of
garden, and you don't know these places exist. And there was
another house in Old Church Road, Kensington. To have half an
acre of open land in the middle of London is fantastic.

A famous name among my group of regular corporate clients
was Tiny Rowland. Whatever people say about him, Tiny
Rowland was a wonderful person. He was a marvellous family
man; he had four children, a wonderful wife and his London pied à
terre was a flat just off Park Lane. I did a lot of parties there, and
we'd sit and chat, afterwards, and have a drink and discuss all
sorts of things. He used to join in the parties, as well. He owned a
hotel in the Edgware Road, near Marble Arch, and the last party he
gave was for all his children – it was a very big party. He invited
lots of people and we organised everything.

Tiny Rowland had strong business connections with Africa. He
knew a lot of African chiefs. There were one or two at the party
and they joined in the 'Musical Bumps' and 'Musical Statues';
they were wonderful. In fact, all of these high-status people are
normal, sociable, friendly beings. It was a pleasure to mix with
them.

My clients were people who had worked very hard for what
they'd achieved and were totally committed to their companies.
They had no airs and graces and they were lovely people. I had a
wonderful life with these people; that's why I enjoyed what I did.

The corporate men would discuss general topics with me,
but not business. With Tiny Rowland, I had shares in one of his
companies, but he wouldn't talk about it. He was very proper and
straightforward.

I met Sir James Goldsmith through his marriage to Lady
Annabel, as I had already organised parties for her when she was
married to Mark Birley. Her brother, Lord Londonderry, was

118

connected with Hammer Films and I showed a Hammer horror film at one of the first parties I did for one of Lady Annabel's children. It was very funny and very frightening, I remember. After that, I organised a party for another of the children, India Jane. The nanny was called Mimi, a wonderful person, and she's still with them, I think.

The Birleys had a superb home, a fantastic house at the back of South Kensington. There's a road of terraced houses that goes between Kensington and South Kensington, with a small opening and you go in there, and behind there, there's an estate. It's unbelievable.

The Birleys had three children: two boys and a girl, and in the seventies, Lady Annabel met and married James Goldsmith. They also had three children: Jemima, Zachariah, known as Zac, and Benjamin, who was known as Ben-Ben. When Jemima Goldsmith was four months old, I organised a christening party at the Goldsmiths' home in Kensington. I provided the food and champagne, the lot.

After that, I did their parties, year after year, the complete parties; entertainment and everything organised. And, as the children grew older and wanted disco parties, I used to get the big disco people down there. In 1999 I organised a summer party for the Goldsmiths at Ormley Lodge with Jemima Khan's little boy, Sulieman.

After the children grew up, and Zac and Benjie went to Eton, Sir James Goldsmith went to America. He had an enormous estate in Brazil and another big estate in Spain, on the Costa del Sol. Pat and I visited them there. We went to this small village, which is now famous for its restaurants; everybody goes there to eat. You go right to the end of village and there's nothing there, just open wasteland and forest. There are two tracks, and one of them leads to Adnam Kashoggi's estate and the other to Sir James Goldsmith's. I think the family used to arrive by helicopter but we drove there for drinks, one day. It's where Princess Diana went for a rest, because it's so private.

Adnam Kashoggi also bought a house in Eaton Square from one

119

of my clients. Then Andrew, now Lord, Lloyd Webber, bought it from Kashoggi. I organised a party for Lloyd Webber's oldest son and daughter, when he lived in Kensington with his first wife.

Lord Hanson and Lord White were famous business partners. Gordon White lived in America most of the time and he married several times. When I first used to do parties for Lord Hanson, he wasn't Lord Hanson. He had a small flat off Eaton Square and he worked from home. I always say it was a pity I didn't get paid by people like him in shares, instead of by cheque. I'd have been happy to have got shares in his company; I'd have been a millionaire, by now! I organised a lot of parties for him. He was very kind and very pleasant. He used to call me 'Uncle Magic'!

A few years ago, I was casting about for job opportunities for Geoffrey. He's got a BA degree in Fine Art, but he can't do anything with it. I wrote to Lord Hanson and said, 'I wonder if you remember me ...' He couldn't help me, but he wrote back, calling me Uncle Magic, and saying how well he remembered me, which was rather nice.

I also did parties for all Gordon White's children by all of his wives. His last child, Luke, like Lord Hanson's boy, is often mentioned in the social columns, and I did their parties for several years.

Although, to all intents and purposes, I have retired from the world of children's parties, a phone call can still prise me from the golf course or a cricket match. It's not so much the parties I miss now, it's the people. I enjoyed mixing with all sorts of people I wouldn't normally have come across. Once upon a time, I used to look forward to every party I was asked to do. But that's finished now. I've done 50 years of parties, and I feel I've done enough. But, strangely enough, once I arrive at a party, once I'm involved in it, I'm back in the spirit of things, as usual. But I don't feel as if I want to get involved any more; I want to relax.

Each party is something you've got to wind yourself up for, like an actor putting on a show. It has to be the best; if not, you're flat or stale. Like an actor waiting in the wings, who is suddenly transformed when he steps out onto the stage, I feel the equivalent rush of adrenalin when I begin my entertainment. When you go through the door and you first see the birthday child, you know if you're going to click or not.

I don't remember not having 'clicked' with a child. But occasionally you get a very spoilt child, but that's usually connected to the parents. This is a relatively recent phenomenon, say, in the last five or ten years, and it's only found in the suburbs, not higher than that. In other words, not the people I entertained in central London.

I attribute the noticeable change in children's behaviour to two things: one is there's a complete laxity in the way children are brought up these days, and, two, as I mentioned before, the standard of entertainment has declined, from what I hear. Parents tell me that some entertainers let the children run wild, and the parents don't want that. So I think there's more than one reason for the change. I don't see any great change in the attitude and behaviour of parents in the areas I mostly worked in in London and the country. But the suburbs are different.

These days, my time is also taken up with a certain amount of voluntary work. This is something I have always been involved in, but now I have more leisure time to devote to various causes and I can relax and enjoy it.

Before the war, I was a member of the Brady Boys' Club and benefited from their organisation. When I returned from the war, Pat and I both did voluntary work as what they call managers at the Club. We used to help out there two or three nights a week, plus the odd weekend or week in the country. We did that from 1946 to 1956 and then my business took over.

It's only in the last year or so, we've been able to go back to voluntary work and help out at an old people's day centre in Golders Green. The name of the organisation is Jewish Care and they run a number of centres; this one is called the Sobell Centre and is named after the philanthropist who gave a lot money to these causes.

Pat and I go regularly on a Thursday morning to help at the centre. It's very interesting, because, although some of them are younger than me, half of them are on sticks or invalids, in some way. They get the whole day there for a very small amount of money. They have coffee and biscuits in the morning, then they go off to various activities, such as discussions or music or dancing, or even T'ai Chi, the Chinese form of exercise. I've been helping a blind chap with T'ai Chi, which I've never done in my life. I sit next to him and tell him what to do.

Then, at 12, about 120 of them sit down to the first of two sittings of lunch. The lunch is like a wedding feast, it's a really magnificent meal. We, the volunteers, serve the lunches and remove the plates and lay the tables again. I've got a video of it; it's like a wedding. And in the afternoon, there's entertainment and tea and cakes, and then the guests are collected and taken home.

There are several of these day centres and they provide a useful service in the community. They have an enormous number of volunteers and they save the organisation millions of pounds.

When Pat came along, she heard they needed volunteers in the hairdressing department, so now she washes the old people's hair. She used to wash her mother's hair, in the old days. While I am downstairs serving teas and coffees and lunches, Pat is upstairs, helping in the hairdresser's. I enjoy helping the people. They're lovely. I see them coming in and I know this one wants a coffee without sugar and the other one wants tea with sugar. I've brought it for them before they've even sat down; they're very pleased and enormously appreciative.

Before I retired, we lived in a large, four-bedroomed house at 80 Bridge Lane, Temple Fortune. We lived there for 40 years and moved there from our flat in Greville Hall, which is where I got the name Greville Films. It's only in the last 10 to 15 years that I've called myself Norman Myers Entertainment, because the clients were calling me Norman Myers. I didn't need the 'Greville', any more.

But, being in the 16-mm film business, of course I owned a 16-mm movie camera. When the children were born, I used to take movies of them and I ended up with an enormous number of films. The trouble was, you had to put up a projector to show the films and people got bored watching them. So in the last ten years or so, everything's gone on video. You send the film away to someone, they put it on video with a bit of music, and all you've got to do is play it in your video machine. I sent away whole reels of old film and now I've got an hour-long movie of my daughter Jennifer, going right back to when she was about two weeks old.

I also have movies of my mother and sister, and my nephews when they were two, three and four years old. I showed a video the other day to the family, and the grandchildren laughed like hell to see their mother as a baby. I gave the film to them, so they can look at it now as much as they like. My nephew in Toronto wants a copy, so I'll try to get one done for him.

Although I was in business, I didn't really collect films myself, except Laurel and Hardy and colour cartoons. But I had to get rid of them all when I moved. I had a good collection, which I sold through the cinematographic journals; I rang someone up and practically gave them away. But I had nowhere to put them. Before, I had a garage and a big room to keep everything in; the films and the party novelties.

But I have held on to other souvenirs. I have many memories of thousands of children and their parents, and they remain as clear and immediate as if the parties had happened yesterday.

9

Fortune's Wheel

Looking back over my career, it is easy to see how and why I moved from organising the rudiments of parties to taking on board every aspect of party needs and entertainment. The cross-over point occurred when Norman Myers Entertainment took over from Greville Films. I started off in my office where I ran the film library for Shell-Mex and BP, a small room next to the Shell-Mex office in the Strand. The complete film department was handed to me, to book films all over the country for people who'd written in, wanting the Shell films shown at their meetings.

I handled approximately 10,000 bookings a year and ran the department for 14 years until a company of American time and motion high priests came along, and the company was restructured. Shell-Mex and I parted company and I acquired an office in Pennine Parade, Cricklewood, relatively close to where I lived. Life settled into a productive and pleasant routine and I could make the most of my full membership of the Royal Automobile Club in Pall Mall.

There are two parts to the RAC Club: there's the men's club in Pall Mall and there's the club in Epsom, where they have a golf course. I used to go to the office in the morning and get everything organised for the parties, deal with the correspondence and make phone calls, then go to the RAC for lunch in Pall Mall and go on to a party in the afternoon.

Even on a Sunday, I didn't desert the RAC. I'd drive down to the club at Epsom and have a round of golf, have a shower and lunch there, and go straight to a party in town. I was working every day. I no longer belongs to the RAC, but I wish I'd kept up my membership a year or two longer than I did. I lost £35,000 by resigning too soon.

The ordinary RAC car breakdown service is separate from the main RAC, which is the private club. You paid several hundred pounds a year membership and you had the use of the club and all its facilities. It's got a magnificent swimming pool and Turkish baths, squash courts and a restaurant, and you can stay there overnight, at a very reasonable price.

I was a member of the club for 23 years. In the last few years, I saw I wasn't using my membership at all. I kept it going for a couple more years, then I thought, it was silly, paying out all this money for nothing, and I resigned from the club. A few years later, the club was sold and the buyers, a big American company, paid every member £35,000!

Talking of fortunes I didn't make, I can tell another tale of bad luck. Many years ago, in 1968, when the property market was booming and you couldn't help making a fortune, I was invited to go into the property business, as a sideline to my main work. I had a friend who was also interested in investing in property, and we had another friend who was a solicitor and had been our best friend for 20 years. The solicitor knew a lot about property and was also keen to invest, and he introduced us to the first investment, an acre of land in Enfield, Middlesex.

The land was very good value for where it was, even in those days. The solicitor suggested the three of us buy the land and form a property company. So we did. And as my friend and I were busy with our own businesses, we remained sleeping partners and made the solicitor our managing director and gave him a cheque book.

We had regular meetings, once a week or once a month, and the company thrived. We built three or four blocks of flats in London, which you can see to this day. Lots of ideas were in the pipeline and on the way to fruition. Then we discovered the solicitor was cheating on us.

Our supposed friend, who was also a member of a trusted profession, was made bankrupt, struck off his professional register and went to prison. But it stopped us dead in our tracks. If we'd gone on, we might have mortgaged our house and lost everything. We were dealing with thousands of pounds' worth of property, which was a lot in those days.

The lucky thing for us was we had one or two properties we'd actually bought outright, and were renting out, and we left them to continue generating income for the next ten or fifteen years. Then, around 1990, when the market was buoyant again, we managed to sell the investments. And that was my pension'

Of course my unusual profession did not provide me with much security. I was self-employed and I'd been badly advised in the past and had to look out for myself. The property company was where we could have made an awful lot of money but we weren't supposed to; we weren't supposed to be wealthy people. Still, there was no need for our friend, the solicitor, to have done that. He could have made a fortune along with us; he was an equal partner. But he was greedy.

The property company and, before that, the magic candle importation scheme; I have always been full of ideas and ready to seize an opportunity.

For relaxation, I joined the Finchley Golf Club, only a mile from my home. I don't have to rush down to Epsom, now, and it was another reason I left the RAC. I started playing golf in 1956. I was playing a lot of tennis and squash at the time – I was a fairly good player of both. I played tennis before the war, and started squash after the war. I started off playing tennis in local parks with friends, nothing serious. Squash, I either played at the RAC or the White House, near Regent's Park and places like that.

A friend had begun to take up squash and I saw a real advantage in the sport. If you're busy, it's a wonderful way of getting exercise in half an hour, instead of in three hours, playing tennis, and I grew to love the game. I played it two or three times a week, and then, in about 1956, my back went. At the time, I was playing tennis with the same friend, and I think we were about 31 or 32. You played games to the bitter end, in those days; you didn't have tie-breaks. At the end of about the sixtieth game, my back went. I've never played since.

My love of cricket and golf have kept me active, both as a player and a spectator, but I have never found tennis interesting as a spectator sport, so I've never queued for Wimbledon tickets.

Golf became my new pastime. I went to Mill Hill and took six lessons. I picked the club up and, although I'm a right-handed person, I play cricket left-handed. The professional said, 'What are you doing?' I said, 'I always hit the ball like this.' He said, 'Well, you've got a right-handed club.' So I was taught to play right-handed, and I've played that way, ever since.

These days, I play golf about three times a week. I'm not very good, but I still enjoy playing. My handicap is about 23, which is not good. I'm not a serious golfer; I only like to play for fun. If I have to play in a competition, I usually play very badly. But I enjoy the game, and I enjoy the exercise. I used to play the full 18 holes but, now I restrict myself to 12 holes. And usually, I use my buggy to go round. I have a petrol-driven buggy, but, unfortunately, in winter, we're not allowed to use it and we have to carry our clubs. So I do nine or twelve holes with about three or four clubs, and wait until the summer to start again.

There's a thriving social side to the Finchley Golf Club which I enjoy. In fact on New Year's Eve, for the millennium celebrations, we went to the club to see in the New Year. We have lunches, we have dinners, Italian evenings, Greek evenings, children's Christmas parties and other social events going on. We also have various sections in the club. I'm in what they call the Senior Section, which is for the over 55s, and we play other clubs, at home and away. If we play the clubs at home, we'll have a lunch or dinner, as well. It's very social, and being so close to us, it's wonderful. It's only five minutes from home.

Finchley Golf Club is one of the best clubs in London. The ground itself is excellent and it's a very pleasant place. I have my own set of clubs and a set of plus twos, rather than plus fours. I found out the reason, the other day, why the trousers are called plus fours: they are four inches below the knee. Plus fours are unusual these days, and plus twos, which are two inches below the knee, are more common because they're not so baggy.

I don't go to the big golf tournaments but I like to watch them on television. However, I won't subscribe to Sky television, so I rarely see the tournaments.

Until a couple of years ago, Pat and I had two or three week's holiday a year in southern Spain, where I spent a lot of time enjoying games of golf with friends on the Aloha course near Puerto Banus close to Marbella. For 14 years, I had a time-share home on the Mijas golf course at Fuengirola for two weeks of the year. I don't use it any more. What I do now is swap the time for various places, either around the world or in England. In fact, I gave two weeks to my daughter and children this summer. They went to Florida and Disney World and they had a magnificent apartment for two weeks. We prefer to stay in England, now, and not just because of my heart by-pass operation.

I wasn't aware I had a heart problem when I visited the doctor's, one day, over 15 years ago. I have no idea what brought it on; I didn't know there was anything wrong. I had to see a doctor for something else and he said, 'You've had a heart attack. We'd better check you out.' Then they said I ought to have a by-pass. I underwent a quadruple heart by-pass operation in 1985. Now I see my specialist every year for a check-up and, touch wood, I'm okay, at the moment.

I'm member of BUPA and I'm glad I joined the scheme 50 years ago. The only trouble is, they keep putting the price up, instead of bringing it down. Subscribing to a private medical scheme, those many years ago, put me ahead of my times. Well, I'm a great forward-thinker. I joined everything, every scheme that was interesting.

The other major sport I'm passionate about is cricket – but in a passive sort of way. I'm a member of the MCC; I have been for over 25 years. I was proposed and seconded by a cousin of mine. Normally, you have to put your name down at birth, if you want to become a member. At the moment, there's about a 25-year waiting list. It's a very good club to belong to. For every test match at Lord's, which is the home of cricket, we have seats in the pavilion. In the last few years, I've been getting reserved seats, as well, which is too wonderful for words.

I see all the cricket personalities there. When Brian Lara, the West Indian cricketer, became famous for scoring three, four, five hundred and he came to Lord's, I was the first one to get his autograph for my grandchildren. In fact, if you watch a match on television, my reserve seat is near the gate where they come in and out, and you can always see me. It's a lot of fun; I enjoy it. I go mostly to the test matches and the finals of certain championships. Playing golf, as I do, I'd rather be active than passive, unless it's a really good game or a test match. Then I'll take sandwiches and spend the day there.

Unlike children's parties, I find the atmosphere at cricket games has hardly changed since I began attending matches. Except in the last year; we've had this terrible fight about admitting women into the club. Unfortunately, we misogynists lost! But the women still have to wait 25 years to join. They're not coming in right away!

Pat doesn't play golf. She thinks it's a slow game. But we're very flexible with our time; Pat goes twice a week to yoga, locally. So, when I go to golf, I either drop her off, or she goes on her own, and we're both free in the afternoons. We play a lot of social bridge. We're not very good players, but we like playing the game. We play three or four times a week with friends. We have about a dozen friends and we divide our time among them. In fact, we can overdo it. Although I am a sociable person, I like to stay home quietly and read my paper or a book, occasionally, and just relax.

Both Pat and I are music and theatre lovers, and these interests take their place beside sport, voluntary work, bridge, holidays, friends and family. Recently we went to a Klezmer concert at the Festival Hall.

Klezmer music is a jaunty style of playing based on Jewish dance music which originated in the fifteenth century in the Jewish communities of Eastern Europe. Groups performed written music at synagogue services and secular festivities and, occasionally, for Christian audiences. I understand this music became popular with people like Gershwin, Cole and Jerome Kern and others in America. In the 1970s, interest revived in

Klezmer music and the style has been taken up by amateur musicians, especially in the United States, performing folk and popular tunes on a variety of instruments. It was a very interesting evening. A chap gave a talk about the subject, and they played different pieces; it was wonderful.

We enjoy going to a lot of concerts, and also to the opera. We go to Holland Park quite often, and we go to the theatre. We only go to matinees because, unfortunately, today being what it is, we don't like going up to town in the evening. You can't park your car and we don't like coming home in the train at night. We go out at three in the afternoon and we're actually back indoors at six. The train service is so wonderful.

We also belong to a number of different clubs. We belong to a society called Jacs, which stands for the Jewish Association Cultural Society. Someone comes along to talk to us every Thursday, and they're extremely interesting people. We had Ken Livingstone the other day, and we were supposed to have had Jeffrey Archer, the day before he fell from grace. We hear people talk on all sorts of things. There are judges, scientists, and we had a Nobel Prize winner; they're all so interesting.

Up to 150 people attend these meetings. We have tea, it costs us 60 pence each, or something ridiculously small. The local hall is warm and pleasant, the committee are nice people and we have a lot of functions where we go out for the day. For instance, we went to the Royal Horticultural Society's gardens at Wisley, we go to the theatre, operas and all sorts of things. We get to know people and they're a good crowd.

I have also been a Freemason for over 50 years. I belong to the Lodge of United Hearts which is the 'daughter' Lodge of the Portsoken Lodge, a City Lodge. It's a very famous lodge. The last Lord Mayor was Lord Levene of Portsoken. I joined the Free-masons in 1948 and was a Master of the Lodge in 1955, I was made an honorary member in 1998 because I'd been a member for half a century.

The idea that Freemasonry is a secret society is nonsense. It's a society with secrets, which is a different thing entirely. In a secret society, you wouldn't say you belonged to it; you'd keep it quiet. Everything about Freemasonry is published these days, but journalists and people who are not Freemasons try to make out it's a bad thing. But it isn't. We're honourable people. We believe in a Supreme Being; we must be loyal and honest to our country and the people who run it. And we don't ask for any favours. I've never had a favour in my life as a mason. People say that because you're a mason, you get preferential treatment from the police or judges, but it's nonsense. The Lodge is simply where the members meet. We never talk business, at all. It's not like the Rotary Club, which is a business club; we're just an organisation and we do certain things.

There is no question that I am a club man: the Freemasons, the MCC, Jacs, Finchley Golf Club, and a past member of the RAC. And I was a member of the Ski Club of Great Britain for years. I've only recently retired from that because their building was at the corner of Belgrave Square and Eaton Square and, three years ago, they sold it and moved down to Wimbledon. Well, I couldn't go down there, it was too far.

I used to ski a great deal, at Grindlewald in Switzerland and other ski resorts. We enjoyed it until my back went, and we don't ski any more. But both of my nephews, in Switzerland and Toronto, are great skiers. In fact, my nephew in Toronto goes to Aspen in Colorado for his skiing about twice a year.

I decided to join the Ski Club of Great Britain, partly because Pat and I were enthusiastic skiers and, partly because the club was situated in my working area in Belgravia. So, if I didn't want to go to the RAC for lunch, I could pop into the Ski Club for a snack or a drink, because it was just off Belgrave Square. The club has talks and group activities, so if I'd wanted to, there was a lot to do, but I never attended the meetings because it meant going back into town at night.

Generally, if we want to go to a music concert, we'll look in the paper to see what's on. But I'm a member of Holland Park, so they send me their brochure every year. They have about six or eight operas or ballets during the summer season. I'm not a ballet fan, but I love opera. Mozart's my favourite composer and *Don Giovanni* is my favourite opera. But, of course, I like *La Bohème* and *The Magic Flute*. I've got them all on CDs and videos. I am a great fan of Maria Callas, the most famous of opera singers.

Reading is another pastime I enjoy but I find I haven't enough time for it. Since we've been in the flat, I haven't read a lot, only newspapers. Before that, I used to read three books a week. I'm a very fast reader. I like thrillers such as those of Robert Ludlum and Wilbur Smith. I prefer light reading, fiction, and I read newspapers from end to end: The *Sunday Telegraph* and papers like that. Years ago, I read all the correct books, if you like; the classics: *Treasure Island*, Dickens and the other authors, and Greek mythology. I'm not a biography reader. Most of these politicians who produce their memoirs, such as *The Crosland Diaries*, Alan Clark and the others, I can't be bothered with them. I simply read the reviews of them in the papers. However, I hope people will like my autobiography!

Art is another subject I am very interested in. Our flat is full of pictures of all styles because I buy art that I like. I don't just buy it to fill a space on the wall.

I have a collection of Don Quixote pictures. I bought an enormous Don Quixote painting by a Spanish artist back from Spain. Then I bought a Don Quixote sculpture, and another Quixote sculpture, then a Don Quixote plate. In America, I bought a Sancho Panza and Don Quixote model. I like the story very much; I like the whole idea of it.

When I had my house, I had three times as many pictures, all over the place. Most of them are in the garage at the moment. Even so, the walls of my flat are crowded with prints and paintings; including Elisabeth Frink and copies of eighteenth-century cricket paintings, and a print by L.S. Lowry. I like pictures, but there's no more space here, so I don't bring anything more home. Well, hardly ever.

The pictures I enjoy are not necessarily expensive. The signed print by the great British artist Elisabeth Frink is an exception. The picture shows three figures on three horses, becoming almost one horse and rider. I bought it quite early on. There was an article in the paper about how prints were going to appreciate and I bought quite a lot. I went to a reputable shop and made some investments in limited editions. But half a dozen of them, I put in the attic in my house, and they're in my garage now.

I bought my first print about 50 years ago, from Athena. The picture hardly looks like a print; the parchment has been painted over in oils and given a beautiful gilt frame. There are others in my sitting room which, at first glance, also look like oil paintings. About 25 years ago, the MCC offered its members six copies of pictures that hang in the Long Room at Lord's. Again, the pictures are on parchment and 'painted up' to resemble oil paintings. They are all cricketing scenes from the eighteenth and nineteenth century and are full of atmosphere and historical interest.

At one stage, I was asked how many parties I have done over the years. I sat down and worked out I did, on average, at least 300 parties a year. Say 40 years, allowing for the fact in the last few years I've cut down the parties to around 200 year, and you can work it out that I have organised well over 10,000 children's parties. There was an article in one of the glossy magazines in 1987, on the fact that I had recently held my 7,800th children's party in Grantham, Lincolnshire.

Another national daily newspaper described me as the Peter Pan of children's parties with a *Debrett*'s-style client list, an entertainer to royalty, aristocracy, diplomats and the wealthy residents of London. Some of the papers gave me double-page spread, but I didn't always know when articles were going to be written about me. Some of them came to interview me at home, or at a party. There was an article in the *Daily Mirror*, where I was photographed with Monty the Monkey and referred to as a quiet man who knows how to make children laugh.

Even the famous magazine editor, Tina Brown, now established in New York, rang me up when she was working for *Punch* magazine and asked to come to one of my parties. I've been meaning to get in touch with her, because she's now one of the top people in New York. She was a cub reporter then and she came with us to one of the parties in Hampstead, but the article turned out to be a little bit sarcastic. Perhaps the young reporter was trying to impress her boss at the time. She is now married to the former *Punch* editor Harold Evans, who continues to work in the publishing business.

I always had a stock of music tapes which I considered ideal for the children to move around to at the parties. But 90 per cent of the disco parties the children go to now have their own tapes, which are terrible. There may be one tune they can jump around to, but the rest of the tunes are boring. But you've got to be diplomatic about it, and, occasionally, it doesn't work. I did a party a couple of years ago for one of these more indulged children. The mother insisted on having a disco. There were about 40 children and not one of them wanted to dance, except the daughter. And the mother would say, every so often, 'You must put this record on, you must put that record on,' and it was very boring for the children.

When I tried to relieve the situation with games and magic, the parents interrupted and the party was spoilt. It rarely happens but I don't like doing disco parties, unless the children are about 11 or 12. Nowadays, they have discos for four-year-olds, which is absurd. Children want to be children, particularly at parties. My parties are traditional, and a lot of parents want a traditional party.

10

The Good Life

Although Pat's grandparents lived in Stamford Hill, Pat herself came from Willesden, in north-west London, an entirely different area to my East End. We're both Londoners, born and bred, but Pat was on the posh side of London and I was in the poor part.

Pat's family history can be traced back through the centuries and is well documented. Among the old family pictures in my office, which is a long room full of cupboards and shelves of paperwork, is a photograph of Pat's greatgrandfather, Barney Aaron (1850–1915), and a picture of a boxer, also called Barney Aaron (1800–59), who was her great-grandfather's grandfather.

The families in Whitechapel, however, were relative newcomers to London. The Jewish immigration started with the pogroms, from Lithuania and places like that. They arrived in their masses in east London at the end of the last century, in areas like Whitechapel. 'Although we lived cleanly, our accommodation wasn't that wonderful. But, gradually as people worked very hard and educated their children and pulled themselves up, so the emigration went from Whitechapel to Hackney, to Stamford Hill, which was very posh, then they moved across to Willesden. Then, as the Jewish people really found success, they moved to St John's Wood and then, of course, to Kensington and Knightsbridge and Mayfair.

All this social mobility happened in less than a century. From about 1890 to about 1960, it took just two or three generations for the Jewish people to move forward. Now, other ethnic cultures have arrived in the old areas: the Pakistanis, Hindustanis and the

135

Bengalis, and they work jolly hard, just as the previous people did, and the families place great emphasis on educating their children. Where the Jewish people lived, in Whitechapel and Brick Lane, it's now all Bengali and Hindustani, while the West Indians are more in south London.

We have lived in our Finchley flat for two and half years now. The move and, most of all, the condensing of all our possessions was a mammoth task. In fact, it was the biggest trauma I've ever had in my life – worse than a wedding. It was terrible. We came into the flat and there were about a hundred boxes; we couldn't move. I nearly cried, it was so bad, but we finally got rid of everything.

We set about taking the doors off one of the bedrooms and making it into a good-sized dining room, and we have put it to good use for all our social evenings. The flat is spacious, with two bathrooms and a good-sized sitting room, but we had been used to a large amount of space in the detached four-bedroomed house we lived in for over 40 years.

The house in Temple Fortune had two gardens, front and back, but I have never been keen on gardening, so I employed a gardeners, but I like to sit in them I'm not active in that direction and I never had time.

Eventually, we were able to fit our best-loved furniture and possessions into our new home. We haven't had to decorate it at all. Everything was done: the carpets were down, we bought the lights and the curtains, nearly all the fixtures and fittings. The only extra furniture we bought was a green chair and a cabinet. Unfortunately, a lot of our old furniture had to go. We had a terrible time getting rid of it. We had to give most of it away. I had tapestries all around the house, about six; I loved them. I had one enormous one in the hall. An antique dealer came along and gave us a reasonable price for them. I just like beautiful things. It was like a museum, taking people around the house. I had lots of paintings. In fact, I gave one painting to a bachelor friend of mine. It's one of these modern nude pictures, and he's got it over his bed!

It was our daughter Jennifer, who suggested the time had come

136

for us to find a more practical home. She said something to the effect of, 'It's about time you moved, or we've got to look after you! You'd better get a smaller place.' I always do as I'm told if I think it's reasonable, and I realised it was sensible advice. Pat agreed with me and we started looking around, and we were very lucky to find our flat.

We have been able to keep up with all our friends. We're in almost the same area and all our friends are within ten or twenty minutes of us. We're a bit further north, but it's nearer my golf course and it's a lot easier. I find West Finchley a very convenient place to live. Wherever we want to go, there are tremendous short cuts. Where we are now, the roads go in every direction. If you want to go on the Heath, or down to the West End, there are short cuts all the way. It's fantastic.

After nearly 80 years of living and working in London, I am familiar with every highway and byway in the city. When American friends come over, I can take them on a tour which they won't be taken on by any of the tour operators. I've lived in London all these years, and I worked in the City for over 20 years, so I know every turning there.

At the beginning of the war, I became friends with a man in the American Air Force. I can't remember how we met. He was older than me, but he had a young nephew who was my age. And so we corresponded, the nephew and I. I sent him my stamp album because he collected stamps, and we became friendly. Then I was sent abroad, so my mother corresponded with his mother, and they wrote to each other right through the war. Then, after the war, we were all still friendly and the family wrote and said a lot of their family and friends were students and were going to do Europe, on bike tours. This must have been in about 1948 or 1950.

We lived in the two-bedroomed flat at the time, and we said if they came, they should come and stay with us. So everybody came and stayed with the Myers. They used to come over, one or two at a time; stay with us for one or two nights, or a week, and then off they went on their tours. Over the years, these friends grew up and married and had children, and they kept saying, 'You must come and see us.' We were invited to a daughter's wedding in Connecticut, and as we'd never been to America, we said to ourselves, 'We must go.'

So we went to Connecticut and stayed with our friends, the Burges, and enjoyed their daughter's wedding. My nephew in Canada came down to visit us, and he was invited to the wedding. He's very friendly with them, as well.

After this first holiday, Pat and I flew on to San Francisco, then on to Los Angeles. We then went to Denver, where some other friends live, and we stayed with them. After that, we went on to Chicago, where we also have friends, and we stayed with them. From Chicago, we returned to Connecticut. So, we met up with friends we'd known since way back and who'd stayed with us, and they reciprocated and we stayed with them, all over America. We were there a month and we had a wonderful time. Since then, we've been back several times. When my friend in Conneticut retired and moved across to San Diego, California, I visited him there, too.

But I never did meet the nephew of my friend in the American Air Force, the man I sent my stamp album to. His name was Cyrus McNinch and his parents lived to be about 95 years old. Cyrus is still alive but I've never met him. After my mother had died, Pat corresponded with his mother.

Pat's marvellous at writing letters. She knows how to say all the right things and she takes care of all our correspondence. She'll send off 30 or 40 Christmas cards and half of the people, I don't know who they are. Some of them are au pairs, because after the war we had nannies and au pairs to look after the children, and Pat's kept in touch with them ever since. They write to her from Sweden and Norway, Denmark and Germany, Spain and all sorts of places.

I never used an agency for our au pairs. It was always by recommendation. We had one and they used to stay for a year and say they had a friend who would take their place. We haven't visited our former au pairs in their own countries but some of them still come to England regularly, and we keep in touch through Pat's correspondence.

*   *   *

Pat is just as active as I am and, apart from her yoga classes and the interests she shares with me, she devotes a lot of time to a Jewish charity organisation called Wizo: the Women's Israel Zionist Organisation, which raises substantial sums of money. She's been chairman of the local branch of that society for about 30 years. She does the job with someone else; there are two of them who share the duties.

Pat chairs meetings for her Wizo branch every two weeks, and she's very busy. It's what keeps us young, really. We're opposites in some ways, but we're well-matched. Pat has the extrovert personality; I'm not so outgoing, strangely enough. When we go out and meet people, I never say a word to a stranger until he speaks to me, whereas Pat will talk to the person next to her and they'll be great friends in ten minutes!

We have travelled a lot over the years, mostly through holidays because my career has kept me working in England and Scotland. But we've always gone on holidays, since the war. In 1948 after we were married, we used to take the car and go away with Pat's parents. We went with them to Majorca and Italy, and we went to Venice, the South of France and Scotland. This was all in the days before package tours and flying. We went everywhere by car, all over the continent Both Pat and I are drivers, so when we went away with Pat's parents we were able to share the driving with them.

Just after the war my father-in-law had a new Singer car and we all drove down to Spain. About a hundred miles from Barcelona, one of the parts, the big end, went. After the war, cars always used to break down. We managed to limp into Barcelona but they couldn't repair the vehicle and, as we were going to Majorca, we put the car on the ferry and sailed overnight. There were only about two hotels on the island, in those days. Now there are about a thousand or more. We stayed in a hotel, high up. There was no promenade in 1947, nothing at all.

We were introduced to a garage owner whose name, when written down, was James Oliver. But it was pronounced Haimie Olivière; the 'J' was pronounced as an 'H'. He told us not to worry about the car and said he would make us a new part. I think all the cars there were running on chestnuts and things like that; there was no petrol about, it seemed, or not much. He took about three days to repair the car, and off we went. We were one of the first tourist groups to go around the island in a car, so we saw everything. After that first trip, we went back to Majorca many times, but we will always remember our first holiday on the island. Many years later, we went back to the same hotel, and I said to the manager, 'I was here in 1947,' and the man said, 'I wasn't even born then.'

Wherever we went on holiday, we found excellent locations. When we went to Belgium with the children, for a month, we rented a house in Knokke, just behind the casino. In fact, we went there a few weeks ago, just to see it again. It must have been about 40 years since we were there. Jennifer was about six and Geoffrey was about two. We put the car on the plane at Southend; the plane would only take two cars at a time, and we flew to Ostend, then drove down to Knokke. I used to commute to work, every weekend. It was a wonderful holiday and we had a lovely house there.

We have also enjoyed a number of cruises. It took Pat 47 years to get me to go on a cruise; I always said 'No,' and she always wanted to go. She'd been on one with her parents, before we were married. But I'd always said cruises weren't for me because I wanted an active holiday. In 1993, Pat finally persuaded me that a cruise would be a pleasurable experience. Since then, we've been on nine cruises. I love them, now! We have cruised the Caribbean, two or thee times, as well as the Gulf of Mexico and the Mediterranean, east and west. We took a May-time cruise in the Baltic Sea, to St Petersburg, and visited the Hermitage. The paintings were magnificent and so was the palace. When we go on these excursions, there's always a guide. On a Caribbean cruise, I bought a camcorder and, since then, I've taken videos on each of our holidays and I've collected about ten. The only places we haven't been to are the Panama Canal and Alaska, but we'll go one day.

We always make friends on our holidays, and often keep in contact afterwards. Pat's very good at keeping in touch with people, especially with Christmas cards. We met this chap,

T. Wilson Goad, last year. He's written three books and had them published in paperback: an autobiography and two others they are full of amusing anecdotes.

On one of our cruises, we sailed in a beautiful 'Princess' liner in the eastern Mediterranean. On the third to last day, met a couple, Ken and Marilyn, probably a bit younger than us, and we became quite friendly with them. This was mainly because the wind was blowing on deck that day, and the chap's sunglasses blew off. I always wear mine on a chain and recommended he did the same. He said he'd never seen that idea before. I had a spare chain in my cabin, so I brought it up and gave it to him. He was thrilled and we became friends from that moment on and made a good foursome for the rest of the holiday.

I gave Ken my address, and two days after we got back, we got a letter from Marilyn, saying how much they had enjoyed their days with us and they hoped to see us again, and it was signed Lord Thomson of Fleet, who's the head of the Thomson organisation. I had no idea it was him. We have remained friends with the Thomsons, and when we were in Canada we looked them up and visited his office. They have a superb art collection, which they showed us, and they took us out to lunch. We received a wonderful letter when we got back, saying how nice it was to see us and they hoped to see us again, and they always send us a Christmas card.

Every year, I meet up with my old friend Trevor Sprake, who I met in 1942 when I was on active service. Trevor is an average adjuster, someone who deals with shipping insurance figures, and he still works regular hours, to this day. Of my wartime comrades, Trevor Sprake is the only forces friend I am still in contact with.

He moved to America about 50 years ago, with his wife and daughter, to whom I'm godfather. She married a very nice chap and they have five wonderful children and live in Miami, and Trevor lives 40 miles up the road, in Fort Lauderdale. Trevor Sprake is probably my oldest friend and we enjoy visiting him in Florida. We write to each other and, when we meet, we simply pick up where we left off without any problem.

We stayed with the family at Fort Lauderdale, in February 1999 and spent a further week in St Petersburg, Florida. Every year, Trevor comes to England, and goes around, visiting all his family and we have dinner together. It's wonderful, the way we've kept in touch.

We decided to have a week's cruise which I'd always said was not long enough, in August 1999 in the Mediterranean. After three days, I caught a terrible bacteral disease called cellulitis, which is the inflammation of cellular tissue. It's nothing to do with cellulite, which is the fashion model's concern. It's bacteria that can get into anyone, anywhere, at any time in the foot, and cause inflammation. It can be quite painful.

For three days, I lay helpless and ill on the ship. I wasn't able to walk, I was on antibiotics, and I was constantly in the care of the ship's doctor, as I was in pain and had to be given painkillers.

It was decided I should return to England as soon as possible. I reached home at half-past one in the morning; at nine o'clock, I was at the doctor's and at ten o'clock I was in hospital, in the isolation ward. I was there for eight days, on a drip, and, after that, I had to take 20 pills a day for three weeks.

This unpleasant experience unnerved me enough to cancel my next cruise, And I've been scared of travelling abroad, ever since. A couple of weeks ago, we did a coach trip, just to Bruges and Amsterdam, but that was near enough to home for me to feel safe. I still haven't got sufficient confidence back to go on a long trip. But I love going away on holiday. We're just off for a week in Leicestershire, but that's not far – I don't want to go far. I prefer to remain close to my own health service, for the time being.

Having travelled hundreds of thousands of miles in my lifetime, and to fairly remote areas, I appreciate I have been lucky with my health, but that cellulitis scared me stiff. I've never had anything like it in all my life, and it worried me. If I'd broken an arm or a leg, it would have been something I could have understood and coped with, but this illness was an unknown quantity.

Like me, Pat loves to travel. She doesn't like long-distance travel too much. This is why, if we go on a cruise again, we'll probably go from Southampton and back again. We don't like flying ten hours, any more, to the Caribbean and back. Just before I caught this cellulitis, we were thinking of going to China and all these places. But we did a round-the-world trip in 1995. It lasted a month and we stayed in five-star hotels everywhere we went – Bangkok, Sydney, Auckland, Hawaii, Los Angeles. So, we've done everything, but without seeing the Great Wall of China or going to South Africa.

Pat keeps in touch with friends over the years, and I am happy to have remained in contact with all the people I met from different walks of life. We kept all the letters we received, for years, until we moved. Then we had to lose them, unfortunately. We had 40 years of correspondence and possessions in the loft; it was heartbreaking to have to part with things.

Ten years before we took the final decision to move, I looked round my home and wondered, then, if it would ever be possible to leave with everything we possessed. I said to Pat, 'Either throw out something once a day, or pack something once a day.' But we never did and it all happened suddenly. Fortunately, we had a very good friend who lived near us and who was a handyman. He sorted out everything in the loft. He packed it all for us. He was wonderful. We couldn't have done it ourselves.

The decisions about what to keep and what to jettison were very difficult to make. We had to be very firm with ourselves; the amount we had to lose was amazing. Some of our possessions remain packed in boxes, even though our flat is crammed with art and mementos. A lot of the paintings are in the garage, and I still have to keep some of my party stuff. I got rid of 90 per cent of it, but I've still got my film equipment and my magic and certain films in the garage. I'll probably keep these things and give them to the children.

Of course I still use my party equipment. I organised two parties for Christmas 1999, for instance, the first one in Swiss Cottage – just an ordinary party for seven-year-olds. I don't even know where they got my name from; I don't need to ask.

I first met Pat when her family lived in Willesden. She was an only child and a friend of my sister, Pearl. It was at her eighteenth birthday party – I had popped in with my sister – that we first set eyes on each other. We were immediately in tune and were married not long after that, in 1947.

Pat soon became involved in my career and our partnership has been a close and committed one throughout the years. With the help of parents and several nannies, starting with Maria, our Spanish au pair, Pat was able to continue helping me after our children were born. Pat's parents lived in the same block of flats. They were upstairs and we were downstairs. They were like detectives, trailing around after Jennifer, keeping a watchful eye on her. Pat's father, who always used to wear a long raincoat, took Jennifer everywhere.

As a result, Jennifer became very close to her grandparents. But, by the time Geoffrey was born, five years later, we were more organised with nannies, the first being Maria.

Jennifer always went to school in London and began at the local school in Temple Fortune. She was in the same class as Peter Mandelson, the cabinet minister. After that, she went on to the Jewish Free School in Camden Town. It was originally in the East End of London, in the nineteenth century. In fact, my father went there in about 1897, and I went there in about 1930, for six months, waiting to go to another school when I got my scholarship. Then my daughter and my son went there, following the family tradition.

Geoffrey went to a private school in Primrose Hill. Then he wanted to go to boarding school, so he went to school down in Sussex. But he wasn't happy there and, after a certain amount of time, we brought him home.

We sent him to a state school in Swiss Cottage. It used to be a fantastic school, called the Quintin Kynastan School. But, under the Labour government, it went comprehensive and everything went downhill. The teaching standard declined and Geoffrey got into bad habits, so we took him away from there and sent him to the Jewish Free School. But, at the end of his time there, we found he wasn't doing very well academically; he was more artistically inclined. We sent him to an art studies school in Kensington for a year, and from there he got a place at St Martin's College of Art, where he got a degree in Fine Art. But he's not been able to do anything with his qualification, which is a great shame. His style is very modern and it's difficult for people to relate to it.

Geoffrey has produced a number of paintings. He sold one to a friend of mine, but that's about all. He doesn't like working for anybody and keeps going by doing odd jobs. He has inherited my need for an independent life – but he should have taken over my business. He could have had a fantastic, ready-made business. He knew it; he used to come to the parties and my clients loved him and he could have made a very good job of it. But it wasn't to be.

Even now, Geoffrey has no inclination to follow in my foot-steps. He valets cars and does decorating jobs, anything to get by. He's content just to make enough to keep body and soul together. He's been in the same small flat for the last ten years. I have to find the rent occasionally! He's not married; he can't afford it. But he's relatively happy, if a little frustrated. I think he'd like to do more on the art side, but there's no future in it. He keeps in touch with the art world and gets the odd teaching job in Hampstead, but it's difficult to sustain. He gets a couple of weeks' work, that sort of thing. An art degree is very difficult to use.

Jennifer took another path – her personality is entirely different. She married a very nice fellow and they've got two wonderful children. She's a very good housewife and mother. She's fairly strict with the children and brings them up properly.

After the Jewish Free School, we sent Jennifer to the Lucie Clayton School in Knightsbridge, where she took a secretarial course. I knew Lucie Clayton, because she was a client of mine, and I knew her children.

Jennifer enjoyed a number of secretarial jobs and worked for me for a certain amount of time before getting married. She met her husband, Michael Bankover, at a social gathering with friends. He'd studied for seven or nine years to be a quantity surveyor and he's now a very good surveyor. For seven years, he was involved in rebuilding the Guildhall in the City. The Queen opened it, and Michael was presented to her. He's done very well and they have a lovely house in Mill Hill.

My grandsons are growing up fast. They're similar ages to Prince William and Prince Harry. Daniel is going on to university after his gap year, doing media studies. He wants to be in television, not on the journalistic side but the technical side. Mark goes to his brother's old school, Mill Hill, and he's very good at sport.

My grandchildren are thrilled when they see me in the newspapers with my photograph. But Jennifer has never let them go to parties with me, unfortunately, because she's always believed that school work comes first. I used to take Geoffrey away from school, so that he could go to the parties, and I think Jennifer went to one or two of my parties, but it didn't interest her enormously. She's very focused on her sons and worries about their future and gets books out of the library to help them. She doesn't let them run around. They've both got computers and they're experts on them. They use the Internet and send e-mails, whereas I can't even programme a video machine! If I get a mobile phone, which I haven't yet, they'll have to show me how to use it.

I am very fond of my grandsons. They're both very good boys. When we go to visit them, which is about every other week, or less, the first thing the youngest boy says to me is, 'Would you like a drink, Grandpa?' He knows I always have a whisky at night at home, and he'll always pour me one. He's very thoughtful; he knows what his grandfather wants.

Since they were small children, I have enjoyed taking the boys out for the day. I've taken them to just about every museum in London. The only thing I can't get them interested in is good music. They're pop fans, and their dad is, as well. And when I talk about my kind of music, they say I'm old-fashioned. It's a shame, because, at their age, I was very keen on music and I had people to help me appreciate it.

Although I can't see anything of my parents in my own appearance or character, I can see my father's handwriting in mine when I write hurriedly. And I suspect I may be like my mother in her

146

sentimentality. She was a very sweet and loving person, like Pat, in that respect. But my parents weren't business people, they weren't organised. They never had the chance in life that we had, but they instilled in me a moral code for living and that's very important.

My children and grandchildren are very different personalities. They're all individuals, even Daniel and Mark, though they're very close and do a lot together. They're both keen on football and Daniel is a Spurs fan. Though Mark is a Spurs fan, he can't afford a ticket so he goes to Watford FC with his father. Mark is very keen on American wrestling. He'll sit up on a Friday night and watch it, and I buy him posters of the sport.

I have lived in London all my life. I wouldn't live anywhere else. When Pat and I return from a trip abroad, we are both happy to be home. We were happy in Bridge Lane, and we're happy here in this flat. We don't know many people here but there are one or two neighbours who live downstairs who we've become friendly with. One of them we play bridge with. He's the chairman of the residents' association. The majority of the flats in this complex are rented out privately. Mostly, they have two or three people living in them, or even more, to pay the rents, and we've no idea who or what they are.

Pat is friendly with our next door neighbours. They look after our post when we're away and things like that. But I don't know their names and probably wouldn't recognise them. I say hello when people say hello to me, and that's it. Etchingham Court is quiet during the day. People are away to business at eight o'clock in the morning, or earlier. The cars go out and come back, and we never see the owners. They seem to be, mostly, professional people, and renting a flat is a reasonable way of living in London; I shouldn't think it's all that expensive, especially when two or three of them are sharing the rent. I estimate that over 60 per cent of the flats have been bought as an investment.

Apart from my hobbies – music, reading, travel, art and sport – I have another passion; I'm a great *Star Trek* fan. I used to read a lot of science fiction when I was younger. Isaac Asimov was my great favourite, because he was an intelligent writer. He wrote *The Foundation*; they were three enormous books and I read them all. Even my nephew in Switzerland, the chap at Cern who's finding out how the earth was formed and smashing atoms, he likes Asimov, as well, so there must be something in him. I no longer read science fiction but I enjoy *Star Trek*, all the same. I love their ideas. I've been watching it for years.

We go to see films at the cinema, occasionally. But no 'kitchen sink' drama – something that's pleasant we enjoy. We went to see *Notting Hill*, and enjoyed that. I have collected all the old musicals on video, all the ones from the forties and fifties, every one you can possibly think of. And I have *Henry V* with Olivier and *Casablanca* with Bogart, and *Oh! What a Lovely War*, which I love and watch quite often. We're going to see it at the Round House soon, and that's the sort of thing we like. I won't go and see anything that's full of bad language. I'm just not interested.

I built up my own entertainment library by taping from the television. As well as the musicals, I've got lots of operas. I've enjoyed watching *Don Giovanni* several times. *La Traviata*, I've got, and *Aida*. So, as well as listening to it on the CD player, I can watch it on television. I regret I don't have as much time as I would like for my tapes and discs. Occasionally, if Pat lets me have a day off, I get a chance to hear them.

I find we rarely watch television these days, except the news at six, seven and nine o'clock. That's virtually the end of it. We don't go to bed early. We enjoy programmes like *Frost* and *Poirot* the Agatha Christie mysteries, *Inspector Morse* and, of course, the classic serials such as the Dickens ones. We don't watch soap operas and we don't watch quiz shows, but we'll watch David Dimbleby's *Question Time* at eleven o'clock, sometimes.

I enjoy a glass of wine with my meal. The trouble is, I'm the only one who drinks it. Pat doesn't drink and Jennifer doesn't drink. My son drinks wine, but he doesn't come here all that often. My son-in-law rarely drinks and when they come over and I open a bottle of wine, they may have one glass. So I rarely drink a glass of wine, except when we go out. Then, I'll order either a glass or a half-bottle. I drink only red wine and prefer the French wines. But I always have a glass of whisky, every night after dinner, for medicinal purposes.

When we go out to dinner and play bridge, which we do two or three times a week, the first thing we do when we arrive is have a drink. Then we sit down and play cards and talk, and we do the same thing when people come here. I don't collect wines but I might buy a half a dozen or a dozen bottles at a time, if it is a wine I enjoy. I use it up when people come. Years ago, we used to give a lot of dinner parties but people don't do this any more. We've all got out of the habit of it now. You go out to restaurants and it's much cheaper now and more convenient. There are no dinner parties any more, hardly any. We only give about two a year.

When I say dinner parties, I don't mean the regular family gatherings with my grandchildren. But, when we invite friends in, they come after dinner and we have sandwiches and cake. In earlier decades, when dinner parties were fashionable, we used to have six or eight, or even twelve people at the table and would go to dinner parties of the same number. It was a lot of work for everybody. We don't do it any more. And that's a general thing. Dinner parties are out, these days. But Pat enjoyed such evenings. She would do a lot more of them; Pat doesn't mind the work. But I said no; it's not necessary any more. People don't invite you back to dinner parties.

11

A Personal View

My two brothers and my sister each had one son. Sidney, who died several years ago, had a son called John, who lives in Israel, but we haven't heard from him for years. We went to John's daughter's wedding in Israel in the mid-1990s but have lost touch with the family since then.

When I first visited Israel, during the war, it was known as Palestine. I went on leave there from Bahrain. I went there again, for a holiday with Pat, after the Suez crisis in 1956, when the new country was well established. A few years later, Pat attended an international bi-annual meeting in Israel for the Women's Israel Zionist Organisation. I went as one of the husbands, and we enjoyed ourselves.

I always enjoy going to Israel and I've been at different times of the year. It's a wonderful place. Most of our friends have got family living there. They're professional people, such as solicitors, or business people, and live mostly in Jerusalem. The standard of living in Israel is as high as in the majority of western countries.

It was in Israel that my sister, Pearl Frances, met a young Frenchman from Sousse in Tunisia. She met him when she went to Israel for six months. They got married out there and went back to Tunis, to her husband's family. Their son, Jacob Phillip, known as Phillip, was named after his uncle and his grandfather, my father, both of whom had died just before the baby was born. He was two months old when my sister brought him to England.

My sister, who was born in 1928, lived in London, apart from the time around her marriage, until she died in 1963. Her husband, Henry, or Nissim as the family call him, was, and still is, a brilliant linguist who can speak and teach a dozen different languages. He's a philologist, and actually knows the basics of languages. But, when he first came to England, the only job he could get was in a warehouse as a clerk. He couldn't earn much money but he and my sister got a house in Herne Hill, in south London. Unfortunately, that's where my sister died.

Phillip Khaiat was only 13 years old when his mother died. Nissim decided to go to Canada with Phillip. The boy was brilliant and went to McGill University when he was very young. He's completely bilingual. His father only spoke French to him and his mother only spoke English. Nissim quickly found a job with the Canadian government. It was a stipulation that all government employees should speak both French and English and Phillip's father was soon teaching French to MPs, civil servants and army officers, and being called 'the headmaster'.

He had this fantastic job for years, and a very good salary and travelled all over Canada. He was in a country that recognised his potential and he blossomed. He is an orthodox Jew but, when he married again, he married a Quebecoise Catholic. She converted to Judaism and she's now quite orthodox. And they have a son, who's my nephew's halfbrother. The couple now live in Ottawa, where Nissim retired and bought a large house. He started his own school there, so he's still carrying on teaching. He had all the right connections and he's got a lovely life.

Phillip now lives in Toronto. He has a highly successful computer business with some very big clients. He's always had his own business, right from the beginning. He's more in software than computer hardware. He doesn't have a large office but his company is very profitable – he drives a yellow Rolls Royce! He likes the elegant things in life. He picks us up in the Rolls and sits there and says, 'Jeeves, are there any messages for me?' and a voice answers him. He has a voice-activated machine he calls Jeeves.

He had a beautiful house built for himself, almost in the centre of Toronto, with a flat above it. We've stayed in the flat; it's a complete suite, and separate. Phillip is very interested in the arts and has connections with the University of Toronto, and goes to all the functions. When we were staying with him, he took us to the university, one night, and the theme was a 'murder' evening. We joined in and, after being given all the clues, Pat and I were the ones who guessed who the murderer was. He happened to be the Chief of Police. We won a bottle of something for guessing it and we had great fun.

Phillip is also a member of various clubs in Toronto and when he comes to England on business, which he often does, he stays at different clubs, such as the Carlton, and takes us to dinner there. He only likes the best. Phillip will pay any amount to secure seats at a Glyndebourne opera and I take him to Royal Ascot. My two nephews take after their uncle in enjoying good music, good wine and good living!

Phillip's married now, with a boy, Jonathan, who's ten years old. He takes his son everywhere. They go skiing in Aspen and they've just been down to San Diego for a holiday, and we've met them in Guadeloupe.

Phillip has always had the latest technology and communicates easily with his cousin, David, my other nephew, in Geneva, Switzerland. They were contacting each other on the internet years ago. They are both so computer literate. At the European Centre for Nuclear Research in Geneva, where David works, they spend millions on one computer.

Dr David Myers is the son of my eldest brother, Leonard Paul. He's a nuclear physicist, and must be about 50 years old, as well. He's the eldest of my nephews. David grew up in Liverpool and went to university there. He married Joan, a medical secretary, in Liverpool and when he qualified, he moved to a post at Cern in Switzerland. They have a daughter and they've lived near Geneva for over 20 years now. Recently, he received diplomatic status because Cern is an international organisation, so he can put CD plates on his car.

David is one of the top scientists at Cern, originally the Conseil européen pour la recherche nucléaire, now the European Organisation for Nuclear Research. It was established for research

152

into subnuclear physics, and has the most advanced facilities of its kind in the world.

David's a brilliant fellow. He works very hard and lectures all over the world: Russia, Argentina, America; he's very modest though. They have a lot of fun trying to find the common denominator for how the world was formed, big bang or otherwise. David has shown me around Cern, which I found fascinating. I didn't understand it all, but it was very interesting!

Like his cousin in Toronto, David has a large house with a separate suite for guests. We visit him quite often and he always has people staying; his mother and, until recently, his father. Paul who died in December 1999, and was extremely proud of his son. He was quite sad that David lived in Switzerland and he couldn't see as much of the family as he would have liked. As you get older, it's more difficult to travel. I think David and Joan will stay in Switzerland. I don't think he'll live anywhere else. The whole family speak French fluently and his daughter is bilingual. He's very keen on mountain climbing and recently, just before his father died, he was climbing in Kathmandu in Nepal. His wife doesn't climb but she plays a lot of tennis and they're very happy together.

David's daughter Lisa has dual nationality and was educated in Switzerland but took her first degree at Sussex University. She had a wonderful time there and qualified in the psychiatric field. Then, instead of taking her gap year before university, she went to China for a year after she'd got her degree and taught English to the Chinese. I think she came back speaking Mandarin. She's now doing her Master's degree in Geneva. She's a wonderful, confident child, and she'll probably work in different parts of the world.

Leonard Paul, my eldest brother, was born in April 1917 and died in December 1999 in Liverpool. Paul had met his wife in Liverpool, where as I've already said, he became a chiropodist after retiring from his career as a sales representative. Paul's funeral was a small, family affair, with his wife, his son David and wife Joan and their daughter Lisa, David's best friend from Liverpool, Joan's brother, who is a doctor in London, and Pat and I and Jennifer.

Fortunately, my brother and his wife had lived in a beautiful, warden-assisted flat since 1994 and my sister-in-law has a lot of friends there. Paul would have been 83 in April 2000. He'd been seriously ill for the last 15 years and, gradually, everything got worse. He had put up with a lot of different ailments. This meant that David spent a lot of time travelling to see his father; flying to Manchester or Heathrow from Geneva in the days before the connection to Liverpool airport.

My other brother, Sidney, was born in 1919. He was 14 months older than me. He was a hairdresser before he joined the war in 1939. Sidney went right through the war; he went to North Africa, Italy, Germany, Belgium, everywhere with the Army. I think he saw a lot of action but we never really discussed where he fought. With each other, we didn't talk about the war. We each had our own way of life, our own friends, our own marriages. When you marry, you establish your own circle and you don't mix as much as before. You see each other at family occasions, but that's about all.

After his divorce, Sidney left the East End for Israel, where he remarried and lived for the last ten years of his life. His son was in the army there. He's a big, tough fellow and he's doing very well out there. Sidney passed away in the early 1990s. He was taken ill and had a short illness and died in Israel.

My sister Pearl did not resemble her mother physically, but the two women had the same sweet nature. She was a very beautiful girl and very tall. She was the tallest of the children, I think.

My parents were not at all concerned with politics but Pat and I follow current affairs closely today. We're interested in politics and we discuss politics, and we've got our views. It's interesting, because Churchill was a fantastic prime minister and he won the war for us. And yet, immediately the war was over, in 1945, everybody voted Labour and threw Churchill out, including myself. We were conditioned by what was being said about the Tories being 'right-wing toffs' who would return us to the old order of things. We'd won the war and wanted to be part of a new society. Labour got a landslide victory, like Tony Blair this time.

But, in two or three years, Labour were shown up for what they were, and I've been a right-wing Conservative ever since. The Labour government only lasted five years and Churchill came back in and the Tories were in for many years.

The massive post-war nationalisation programme of key British industries, such as coal-mines, docks and harbours, was not to last. The whole thing was a flop. It was a con. It cost us a fortune and it's still costing us a fortune. That's why I was so pleased when Margaret Thatcher broke the unions. Through my own experience, I believe you have to work for what you get.

I have mixed feelings about the National Health Service. As far as I'm concerned, although I have private health insurance, I think what they do for Pat and me is wonderful. What they did for my brother Paul in Liverpool was absolutely disgraceful. I think they killed him, but that's another story. The last four weeks of his life were terrible. You read about it in the papers: how they're starving the old people, not bothering about them, and that's what they did to my brother. I know, for a fact, they neglected his needs.

Paul was in and out of hospital many times during the last weeks of his life. They never fed him, they never had the proper equipment and they left him alone a lot. When I went up there, thinking he was on his deathbed, he bucked up and was cheerful enough. We took him home and went back to London. The next day, he wasn't well and I arranged for a private doctor to see him. As soon as the doctor saw my brother, he rushed him back into hospital. They kept him on a trolley for about ten hours, then put him in a deserted ward, freezing cold with no one to look after him. And then he died. I think it was the most terrible thing.

What was distressing was that my brother was aware of his mal-treatment. He was furious, and he was crying because he was ill. My nephew is going to write a very stiff letter to the authorities, for what it s worth.

But I've had a different experience of the NHS in London. As far as Pat and I are concerned, they couldn't look after us any better. We're registered with a clinic here, in Finchley, and they're marvellous to us. I think it's the luck of the draw with the area. In Liverpool, they've closed nearly all the hospitals. Now I believe there's only one and they don't have enough staff there.

155

There's a lack of resources and the people who run the area don't seem competent.'

Peering into the future, my hope for the generations of my family to come is that everyone should be able to live out their lives as they want to, and not interfere with other people. That most famous phrase, 'Do unto others as you would they should do unto you', was a Jewish phrase, and nothing can beat that.

I am now the only surviving child of the Myers family who lived, worked and played in Whitechapel. I am fit and well, and full of enthusiasm for all the hobbies and interests I have, and touch wood, I've had no complications from my heart surgery 15 years ago. I've been active and sporty since I was a child and this has probably contributed to my good health today. The cycling across England, the running around the London streets, the tennis and squash and the golf have all helped to keep me in good shape. As I enter the new millennium, I am in my eightieth year, but I'm told I look at least a decade younger.

If I live to my eightieth birthday we'll celebrate just as we celebrated our golden wedding on 8 September 1997 with 70 people at my golf club. That was wonderful; they looked after us very well, with the family and the children. My nephew Phillip took a video of the evening, so we've got a record of it to put with our other big occasions.

I have never really been a smoker. I smoked a cigarette occasionally during the war and a pipe when I came out, which seemed to be the thing to do. Then I smoked cigars: I used to smoke one big Havana cigar every night with my glass of whisky until I had my heart by-pass op. The doctors told me not to smoke and, for 15 years, I ve cut it out completely I had no problem giving up my nightly cigar. If I do somethlng, I do it 100 per cent.

My father always smoked a pipe and my brother smoked a pipe until he died. I remember my father as being an impractical sort of man. He had no ambition. Any ambition he may have had was crushed in him when he was young. When I knew him, he simply sat in his chair and read a paper. My mother was the one who was active all the time. My father was so frustrated at having had so little education that he gave up. He married late in life, had four children and somebody to look after him.

Phillip Myers, my father as I've said, was one of 13 children in a family that came from Manchester. We met some of the family when we were very young, but I can't remember much about them. Pat and I have kept in touch with the daughter of one of my cousins, the granddaughter of one of my father's brothers. We haven't got many relatives on that side but we're very great friends with her. She lives in Stanmore, Middlesex, and has lots of children and grandchildren and we see her quite often; she has a wonderful family.

It is Pat who has been my pillar of support for over 52 years. She will always talk to people, whereas I will hang back and speak only when I'm spoken to. I'm a different person at a children's party. Once I'm with the children, I don't see or hear any adults at all. I only see and hear the children for the whole time I'm there. Some entertainers tell me they don't like adults in the room because it disturbs them. It doesn't worry me, I don't even notice an adult, I'm concentrating so much on the chiidren. When I'm at a party, I put on a kind ot cloak, or take off a cloak. I slip into my 'Uncle Magic' mode and enter another world.

Vic is the only entertainer I still keep in touch with. Some of them have died, some of them have moved away and some of them have disappeared.

I see myself as neither a leader nor a team player in life. I'm an organiser of children's parties and I am, I think, a first-class entertainer. It has always been like this, since my early days at the Brady Club; I am there, one person on my own, organising and entertaining.

Although retired, I will agree to do a children's party if someone telephones me, but I keep the price reasonably high. And I'll do any charity parties that come up. But I don't advertise any more, I don't push it any more, and I don't particularly want to do it any more. Ninety per cent of the people who ring me now, don't come back to me the following year. Which pleases me, these days. There are so many hundreds of entertainers now so much cheaper than I am, there's no probiem with the market.

Not only do I collect paintings but I love, books on art, as well. I have an interesting book on posters by David Hockney, one of the greatest artists of the twentieth century. His is the sort of art I like, even though I don't like modern art. I bought the book when I went to an exhibition of Hockney paintings. I also have a book on Dali posters. I'm not a Dali fan, normally, but we were in St Petersburg, Florida, in February 1999, where Dali opened his own museum, and saw the most wonderful exhibition of paintings. We were taken round and I was impressed when they explained all the ideas in his pictures. The museum itself was impressive, and so were the paintings.'

When it comes to art, I prefer, the old masters, as a rule. We went to the Monet exhibition in 1999, and the Rembrandt exhibition and we've also been to the Van Dyck exhibition. They were all wonderful and absolutely the kind of art I like.

My favourite periods for paintings are the 1500s and 1600s. I'm fond of the Italian masters. I've been to Italy many times, to the Uffizi in Florence, and I've been to Venice and to Rome. Until recently, I always made a bee-line for works of art and places of architectural interest when I was on holiday. I don't any more, though I feel I've done enough churches and museums. Last year, I enjoyed the Basilica in St Peter's in Rome; I've been to the Vatican before and the Sistine Chapel and I was impressed. But we'd just been to Bruges and gone through the churches there. Last August, we were in Seville and went to the cathedral; it was absolutely out of this world and I've got a video of it. But, for now, I have seen enough. I used to take Geoffrey to a great many art exhibitions, which may have been where he first became interested in art as a career. He also grew up in a house full of art. Every space was either tapestries or pictures. But he likes Hockney and the modern painters. He has an entirely different taste in art to me. Strangely enough, he made me buy the Lowry print; he saw it in a shop and told me to buy it. I think it cost me about £150. And he recommended another one, I can't remember which one, but most of my pictures I chose myself.

As well as pictures and books, our home is full of photographs of friends and family and ourselves on holiday, thanks to Pat. She likes hundreds of photographs.

Now we dress casually. I'm not a modernist; I have some suits that are 20 years old and I still wear them. I don't like going out to buy new things, if I can help it. When I first organised children's parties, I always wore a suit. Now, I wear a pair of blue-green trousers. When I arrive, I'm wearing a jacket and, maybe, a pullover. As soon as I get there, I take off the jacket. In this way, I feel, the children are looking at colour as well as movement. I'm very informal, I don't dress up as a clown. A lot of clients ask me if I'm going to wear a costume and I tell them my parties are very traditional I find children are more relaxed with that sort of party. A lot of children are scared when a clown comes in.

But I have been Father Christmas many times. One of the most amazing parties I did was for some very wealthy people in Kensington. The secretary rang me and asked me if I'd be 'Mr Holly'. I said, 'Who's "Mr Holly"?' And 'Mr Holly', evidently, is the one who introduces Father Christmas.

I took my Father Christmas costume to the part, but the clients wouldn't let me wear it. I had to wear a 'Mr Holly' uniform, which was green, and they supplied me with an enormous throne. They were very wealthy people, as I say, and money was no object. I had to sit on this throne and receive the children before we could even start playing games. It was amazing.

When I was Father Christmas I used to go round the children, asking them what they wanted for Christmas. But this 'Mr Holly' was something I'd never done before. Years ago, I would ask the children if they'd been good during the year. But you don't do that today, and you're scared to touch them. I usually arrange for someone else to be Father Christmas; Uncle Vic, or someone like that.

Looking back over the last half century, it has been an exciting and rewarding time during which I have built up an unusual and special career. I think I've given a large number of children enjoyment and satisfaction, and satisfaction to the parents; they've had me to do the parties for their children the way they've wanted them done, and everyone's thoroughly enjoyed them. The children have been happy to have me, and we've been to the weddings of some of these children, Pat and I, in Oxfordshire and at St James's Palace and different places.

These wedding invitations have been one of the many kinds of feedback I have received over the years. I was determined the parties should be a success and was happy that they were a success, and delighted that we'd completed the party without any problems.

I always took great pride in my work. I aimed for perfection all the time, but, at the same time, keeping things in the right spirit of the party for the children. I have a rapport with children; we seem to click. The children are always my priority. There are not many entertainers, even today, who can entertain three-year-olds for two hours, which I do.

My concern is that the children are kept amused and they don't get out of control. One wants to make sure they enjoy themselves and one doesn't want to be too strict. You don't want to be like a school teacher when you go to these parties; you've got to have a feeling for the children. The children are my clients, quite as much as their parents.

If the children are five years old, or under, I will produce a bright red egg to interest them. If the child is shy, or crying, when I open this, the child is so surprised, he stops crying. When the child attempts to take the egg, it disappears. When the child blows, the egg reappears. It's a very good ice-breaker for any party. The child realises he's in for some fun and we carry on.

At one stage in my career, I had cornered the market in children's parties. I knew no one, at all, who was entertaining children. I was so busy and I had such an impressive clientele that, as far as I was concerned, there was no one else doing the same thing. Then I met some friends who were members of the Magic Circle. They invited me along to the Circle and, lo and behold, I was sitting at the table with 20 or 30 children's entertainers! That was the first time I realised there were other entertainers out there.

I have met one or two famous entertainers. I met Paul Daniels at the Magic Circle and the House of Commons children's parties. One chap I recommend a lot, if I'm asked to do an adult party, which I never do, is Alan Shaxon, who was the international president of the Magic Circle. He's a wonderful chap and we're great friends and I've been happy to pass a lot of work to him, especially New Year's Eve parties and events like that.

Until last year, I provided a different Magic Circle entertainer almost every New Year's Eve for a certain restaurant in Chiswick, and the owner was very happy about this. I recommended Alan twice, and another chap twice, but all the others were different each time. The owner retired last year, so I don't need to do it again.

I became a magician myself because I saw someone performing and I didn't like what I saw, and I began to build up my repertoire. I never joined the Magic Circle, as I never liked to join professional organisations. I do 40 minutes' magic for children but I don't profess to do adult magic. I'm quite happy doing what I do for the children.

I can't remember where I picked up my magic tricks; I certainly never scoured magic shops. I've been into magic shops recently, with my grandchildren; they've been interested in magic but they're more interested in magic card tricks. And they're very good at it – they fool me. I wish they were ten years older; they could have taken over the business.

It was a fantastic business, and I would have liked to have passed it on to a member of my family. But it's one of the few businesses that has no assets, except goodwill, which is me. If I had a shop or any other sort of business, I might be able to sell it for quite a large sum of money which would keep me going in my old age. But this business was based on me, personally, so the value ends when I stop working.

When I took Geoffrey to parties, he would take the party photographs. And he was a very good photographer. He earned quite a bit of money, I remember. He took about 60 photographs and had them developed and took them to the client and made the sale. Geoffrey met all the top people through his work with me. They loved him, but it didn't work out. He just wasn't interested. He was drawn to art rather than live entertainment, and there it ended.

161

* * *

One of the people I most admired is a man who came to the Brady Club when I was 13 years old. He was the Honourable Philip Samuel. In those days, he must have been about 30 years old, and I looked up to him tremendously.

The Brady Street Club was at a very low ebb, almost finished, when Philip Samuel came to help out. He was a university man and a very quiet sort of fellow, interested in art and music and books. He used to come to the Brady Club before the war and look after the library, and we became very friendly and kept in touch. He helped me to appreciate literature and music.

In later years, when he moved to a retirement home in Eastbourne, even then, he would come up to London on his own and stay with us. I knew him for over 60 years.

Philip Samuel's family were connected with the Shell Oil Company and, at the beginning of the war, Philip was sent out to Hong Kong to work in oil. He was taken prisoner by the Japanese very soon and remained in captivity throughout the war. We used to keep in contact through his mother. Every six months, she would send a card to his friends, and she would receive a postcard from him, once every six months. After the war, he was able to return to England.

When we went on holiday to Hong Kong, Philip gave me a letter of introduction to Lord and Lady Kadoorie. They owned a large part of Hong Kong and Philip had worked for them, just before war broke out. When we arrived at the hotel in Hong Kong, there was a large bunch of flowers and a bottle of champagne from Lady Kadoorie, who then invited us to visit them at their estate in the country and join them for a concert. Unfortunately we didn't have time to go, but it was the sort of thoughtful invitation that I remember Philip for.

Philip would often stay with us at our house in Bridge Lane. When he died, I was shocked to discover he'd left me £500. I'd never dreamed, in a million years, he would do something like that. He was a charming fellow.

By a twist of fate, the doyenne of English nannies, Nanny Ellis, retired to Eastbourne, too. The Airlies bought her a small flat; she

162

still lives there and we keep in touch. I introduced her to Philip, and they used to meet up. There was no question of romance, he was 20 or 30 years older than she, but he would take her to his club and they enjoyed themselves. Pat and I would go down there and see them both.

My mother was, undoubtedly, the greatest influence on my life, with her attitude of hard work and organisation. She influenced me in the way I was brought up and my nature and approach to life. I had great respect for my father but he was a negative man and my mother influenced me much more. When my father died in 1951, nearly fifty years ago, she stayed in the flat in Hackney and died seven years later. I don't know how she felt about losing my father; I wouldn't like to say. I'd left home and was married, by then.

I don't think luck has played a major part in my life. I haven't won the lottery, so there can't be any luck in it! My philosophy is 'life is what you make it' and I am a self-made man. The magic candle importation problem and the property partnership venture were bad luck, but I've got to thank God for the way we got through it. I've been proud to meet people and I only wish my mother had lived to see us make a success of our lives. She saw the very beginning, in the fifties, but she saw hardly anything. I probably still had two jobs then. She would have been so proud of my first car. In those days, nobody had cars; not in our circle. I also regret I didn't have the chance to take my mother on holiday. I think, in all her life, she only went to Paris for one day with my late sister. I've still got her passport, somewhere.

But I had no idea, when I began my business, just how successful I would become. I didn't see where it was going; it just grew and grew. The amazing thing is, it began at the top, whereas, normally, you expect to start at the bottom. I started with a lot of top people and it carried on from there.

After organising the first party for Ralph Richardson, it was only a question of time before other top people asked for my services. I was impressed, meeting these people; they were very important in those days. Richardson was at the height of his fame, and to go into the houses of people like that was amazing. But, the interesting thing is, I never felt overawed by them, I felt completely at home, sitting down and having a drink and a chat with them.

In the last few years, with Pat coming with me now, we finish the party and pack up and leave. Social life has changed, and life's much busier for people, these days. There's very rarely a drink afterwards. We're away in five minutes. But if I'd done that 20 or 30 years ago, I wouldn't have had any business. Of course, the parents of the children are much younger than before. If they knew my age, they wouldn't have me. Let's be honest about it, who's going to employ a man of nearly 80 to entertain children? I'm sure the people I'm doing the parties for next week have no idea how old I am.

I don't consider myself to be a deeply religious person, but I do believe my religion has shaped my life to some extent. Morally speaking, though, I try to live up to the standards it sets. And my friends are about as religious as I am. We go to the local synagogue about once a month – more often than we used to because Pat likes going and the service is very good, not boring. We used to go about twice a year. The average Jew only goes to the synagogue two or three times a year, on the important days: Rosh Hashonah and Yom Kippur, the New Year and the Day of Atonement. Our New Year, Rosh Hashonah, is around September and, for ten days afterwards, we have the ten days of penitence. And, on the tenth day, I suppose like Catholics, we confess our sins and ask God for forgiveness.

The Day of Atonement was the day the Egyptians invaded Israel, over the Sinai Desert, and hoped to smash the country because everyone was expected to be at the synagogue for the most sacred day of the year. That's why it was called the Yom Kippur War.

The Egyptians, however, were wiped out. In fact, the Israelis got as far as just outside Cairo, and it was only because the Americans said 'Stop' that they stopped. And the Americans gave the whole of the Sinai to the Egyptians – anything for peace.

164

* * *

Having lived in London all my life, I haven't consciously noticed the changes that have taken place in the city over the decades. One thing, though, whether or not it's because of the newspapers and their reporting, London sounds a more dangerous place, these days. Years ago, people used to go out in the evenings but now we rarely go 'up town', and if we do, we come back very early. We don't wander around – but that's happened all over the world. Morals are much more lax these days, with drugs and God knows what. There are so many things going on, muggings and the like, that you try to keep yourself to yourself.

One very big change in London I have noticed is that more people have got more money. But Pat and I live in a small social circle. We have lots of friends similar to us and we don't mix with people outside that social sphere, except when I do parties, and that's an entirely different matter. We don't watch television 'kitchen sink' dramas or soap operas, or anything like that, because we're not interested in that way of life. We don't like to hear bad language or see sex on television. We're straight-laced people, if you like; we always have been and our friends are the same. So I can't really comment on the way people live, socially, except for what I see in the newspapers and on the television.

I think television is the worst thing that's ever happened to people and the Internet is going to be even worse because it brings communication from all sorts of people, the very young to the very old, without any controls or censorship whatsoever. I think it's a Frankenstein monster that's grown up from the American idea of communication and it's going to be very sad.

My grandchildren are computer literate and mobile phone orientated. It's a different generation and a different outlook and we are, in a way, left behind. I think every generation is the same. Every parent says, 'We didn't do this, or that, in my day.' But in the last hundred years, progress has escalated so fast, it's unbelievable. And I think, in the next ten years, it's going to be even faster than it is today. Communications are becoming amazing.

* * *

Retirement means I can relax much more than I ever did before. I'm not worried about the parties any more, and we're satisfied and happy with what we've got.

In the past, the parties had occupied a large proportion of my thoughts: as soon as one party was finished, I was thinking about the next one. One had to organise everything, especiaily if one was doing several parties a day. One had to work out all the details.

I used to write out timetables with military precision. Everything was written down. For instance, my records for a typically busy few days in 1965 give shorthand details of the kind of arrangements I had to make, such as 'Vic collect' some important item. On the Sunday, I was organising four parties. On the Saturday, there were eleven parties to organise. It all had to be worked out, it wasn't always easy. I was constantly racing against the clock. I had to work for everything we have. Nobody's given us anything, except Pat's father lent us £50 to buy a van for the business. He lent us the money, he didn't give it to us. Today, I give the children money, but we both think Pat's parents had a good philosophy. They weren't wealthy, but they weren't poor. If I needed money, they'd lend it to me, which gave me a sense of responsibility. I've no complaints about that. When we went on holiday with them, we split all the expenses, the food and the petrol, everything, right down the middle.

Children, now, have too much laid on for them and it's all passive, like television. Too much rubbish and pap. When you think that most kids watch these soap operas which don't show reality or what's really going on in life. But people believe these programmes; but there you are, we're square!

I still call the Brady Club my university. Nobody ever forgets their roots and no one should ever be ashamed of their roots. The club taught me how to live with my fellow men, the importance of good manners, the joy of music, theatre and books. I believe the club got the best out of people, teaching them the power of organisation and how to think things through in advance, all of which have helped me through the war years and on to my career.

On Remembrance Sunday, every year in November, when I attend the Brady Remembrance Meeting, the club calls out the names of former boys who were lost during the war. We meet at a club in Edgware, called the Brady Maccabee. This club has taken over the club in the East End because most of the Jewish people have disappeared from Whitechapel now into other parts of London. It's a boys' club still, and does a lot of communal work, but it's not the same as it was in our day. The children there are entirely different.

The old Brady boys still meet at the Edgware club, coming together to remember their lost comrades. There are usually about 50 or 60 of us. Some of them, we haven't seen for donkeys years and it's interesting to see them again. The names of the war victims are read out, followed by a short service. There's a plaque that was designed by the same chap who created the Olympic Games symbol. It's a beautiful thing with the names of the Brady boys who died during the war on active service.

A former Brady girl reads out the names of the girls who died, whether on active service or not, and the list includes the names of the boys who died when the last V-bomb of the war fell on Hughes mansions in Vallance Road in the East End. After that we talk together, like any reunion, and it's good to meet again.

Looking back, I couldn't have done it without Pat. She's been a help to me for 52 years. We disagree on everything; apart from that, we get on very well together. The only thing that upsets me is when we play bridge. We play opposite each other, as opponents, and she always gets the most fantastic cards, and I don't. She's called the best card-holder in Golders Green, but don't tell her that!

Time has rushed by at an incredible rate. It amazes me that it's been fifty years. It's gone in a flash. I can't believe it's been five decades. But I am not sure I would like to put the clock back to those hectic days. When I say I'd like to be 20 years younger, I don't know if that's true or not. I'd like to have another 20 years to go, as I am now. And who knows?

I like to go on lots of holidays and I'm enjoying life with my family and watching my grandchiidren grow up. During my working years, most of the people who were anybody in England were my clients, and they appreciated me. I've got the satisfaction of knowing I did a good job and I've enjoyed every minute of it. That's what's important.

APPENDIX

My children's entertainment was always *traditional*. As mentioned before, I made sure I arrived at least 30 minutes before the party started. If the party started at 3.30 p.m. I usually rang the front door bell at exactly 3 p.m. (I was usually parked nearby for at least 10/15 minutes before that time). However, if I were asked to provide my large balloons I arrived 1 hour before (I used a vacuum cleaner which blew out at one end). If I had to do the catering too I arrived with my staff at least two hours before.

For a normal party, say for children from 3 to 7 years old, when the children arrived I would greet them with the birthday boy/girl, (who I immediately became friendly with on my arrival.) The first thing I did was to play a little game with the children even if only two or three children were there. If very young – say 3–4 years old – I made a small circle and played 'Here we go round the Mulberry Bush' for several minutes, never persuading a child to join in unless they wanted to or with their mother or nanny. After that, the ice being broken, I put some music on for them to jump for Musical Bumps. This and Musical Statues are the favourites of all children aged 3–7 (7–9 year-olds also enjoyed these games). I varied the way I played these games so as to appear slightly different to the basic games. With the very young I usually gave a small prize to the one who sat down first but eventually all the children taking part received a prize. Either a delightful 'ring' for a girl or a little dinosaur toy or similar for a boy. After a few minutes I would join the individual children in twos then in fours and so on until all the children were joined up in a circle. I would then ask the birth-

169

day child to go in the middle of the circle and we would play 'The Farmer's in his den'. This is a great favourite for 3–7 year olds. We start with singing the 'Farmers in his Den' (all the children sing as they go around in a circle). Next we choose someone to be the wife, then the wife wants a child, the child wants a nurse, the nurse wants a dog (at this stage when we say the word 'dog' every one has to bark like a dog). Someone is chosen, we follow with the dog wants a bone. Then the dog wants a cat (every one miaouws), the cat wants a mouse (everyone squeaks), then finally the mouse wants some cheese and we all say 'oh dear'. By this time we have two circles with the dog and the bone kneeling in the middle. To finish the game we used to say 'we all pat the dog and the bone.' However, I found with older boys it got a little rough so I used to substitute 'We all *clap* the dog and the bone'. As I mentioned before, Prince Andrew was at several of my parties and cheekily he always chose me to join him in the middle, whatever the character was at that time.

As the children are now still in a circle I sit them on the floor to play Pass the Parcel. My game is slightly different to the normal as I enclose a little prize inside each wrapper (I never use sweets either in this game or any time in my parties, except for Smarties in a magic trick at the end of a party). I put the music on. As the music plays the parcel is passed from hand to hand, when the music stops whoever has the parcel in their hands opens one sheet and keeps the prize. However he or she must now do something to earn that prize. If the children are very young (3–5) I ask them to stand up and sing a nursery rhyme. Most of them know 'Baa Baa Black Sheep' or 'Humpty Dumpty'. It is amazing how even the shyest child would happily stand up on their own and sing a song. I usually arranged for the birthday child to receive the last present, which was usually something rather good. And I would say 'Happy Birthday, this is your present.' I might finish the game with Musical Statues if there is still time before tea, otherwise we all trooped into tea with the birthday child leading their friends. It was always very important, without showing too much favouritism, to allow the birthday child to feel very important at their own party.

I stayed with the children all the time they had their tea and made sure the ceremony of blowing out the candles and cutting the cake and all singing Happy Birthday went off traditionally. Especially as I always produced my magic candle which was a lot of fun.

After tea came the 'loo' and washing of hands and face. I always made sure an adult stood by the door with a damp cloth to wipe their sticky hands and faces before going into the drawing room or wherever.

After tea I then did my Magic Show, once again the birthday child helped me most of the time, with his friends joining in when extra help was required. I then finished off with 'Monty the Monkey', my large puppet, and they usually sang together at the end. I then asked all the children to say 'Thank you' to the birthday child, who then gave out their 'Going home' presents and that was that.

For older children the format was the same, i.e. games and competitions before tea, magic show after tea. If a disco was requested the games and competitions would consist of or include dancing competitions. Also after tea we finished with the final dancing competitions and with the birthday girl and I as judge gave a delightful present (usually an Indian necklace or similar) before the magic show. I had games and competitions for every age from 3 years old to 14 years old, both for boys and girls.